# Cambridge Elements

Elements in Creativity and Imagination
edited by
Anna Abraham
*University of Georgia, USA*

# CREATIVE AGENCY UNBOUND

Ronald A. Beghetto
*Arizona State University*

Maciej Karwowski
*University of Wrocław*

Shaftesbury Road, Cambridge CB2 8EA, United Kingdom

One Liberty Plaza, 20th Floor, New York, NY 10006, USA

477 Williamstown Road, Port Melbourne, VIC 3207, Australia

314–321, 3rd Floor, Plot 3, Splendor Forum, Jasola District Centre, New Delhi – 110025, India

103 Penang Road, #05–06/07, Visioncrest Commercial, Singapore 238467

Cambridge University Press is part of Cambridge University Press & Assessment, a department of the University of Cambridge.

We share the University's mission to contribute to society through the pursuit of education, learning and research at the highest international levels of excellence.

www.cambridge.org
Information on this title: www.cambridge.org/9781009479431

DOI: 10.1017/9781009479417

© Ronald A. Beghetto and Maciej Karwowski 2025

This publication is in copyright. Subject to statutory exception and to the provisions of relevant collective licensing agreements, no reproduction of any part may take place without the written permission of Cambridge University Press & Assessment.

When citing this work, please include a reference to the DOI 10.1017/9781009479417

First published 2025

*A catalogue record for this publication is available from the British Library*

ISBN 978-1-009-47943-1 Hardback
ISBN 978-1-009-47945-5 Paperback
ISSN 2752-3950 (online)
ISSN 2752-3942 (print)

Cambridge University Press & Assessment has no responsibility for the persistence or accuracy of URLs for external or third-party internet websites referred to in this publication and does not guarantee that any content on such websites is, or will remain, accurate or appropriate.

For EU product safety concerns, contact us at Calle de José Abascal, 56, 1°, 28003 Madrid, Spain, or email eugpsr@cambridge.org

# Creative Agency Unbound

Elements in Creativity and Imagination

DOI: 10.1017/9781009479417
First published online: September 2025

---

Ronald A. Beghetto
*Arizona State University*

Maciej Karwowski
*University of Wrocław*

Maciej Karwowski was supported by a grant from the National Science Center, Poland (2022/45/B/HS6/00372).

**Author for correspondence:** Ronald A. Beghetto, Ronald.Beghetto@asu.edu

**Abstract:** Creative Agency Unbound explores how individuals transform creative potential into creative actions. Creative agency refers to the self-directed capacity to envision and enact meaningful changes within contextual constraints. This Element introduces the updated Creative Behavior as Agentic Action (CBAA) model, explaining four key decision points that shape creative engagement: Can I do this creatively? (creative confidence), Should I do this creatively? (creative centrality), Will I do this creatively? (creative risk-taking), and How will I do this creatively? (creative self-regulation). Each decision and its related self-belief is discussed in successive sections, integrating theory, research, and practical applications to illustrate how creative self-beliefs motivate creative behaviors. This Element serves as a foundational resource for those seeking to understand, study, and foster the transformation of creative potential into creative action.

**Keywords:** creativity, creative agency, creative self-beliefs, creativity research, creativity theory

© Ronald A. Beghetto and Maciej Karwowski 2025

ISBNs: 9781009479431 (HB), 9781009479455 (PB), 9781009479417 (OC)
ISSNs: 2752-3950 (online), 2752-3942 (print)

# Contents

1. What Is Creative Agency and Why Does It Matter?   1
2. Creative Confidence: Can I Do This Creatively?   10
3. Creative Centrality: Should I Do This Creatively?   20
4. Creative Risk-Taking: Will I Do This Creatively?   27
5. Creative Self-Regulation: How Will I Do This Creatively?   37
6. Creative Behavior as Agentic Action: Theoretical Propositions   52
7. Supporting Creative Agency: Practical Questions and Strategies   64

References   72

## 1 What Is Creative Agency and Why Does It Matter?

This section introduces our conception of *creative agency*, building on our and others' previous work on creative self-beliefs and our updated model of *Creative Behavior as Agentic Action* (CBAA). Our goal is to describe its role in understanding how individuals convert creative potential into meaningful action. We begin by examining the philosophical foundations of human agency before offering our definition of creative agency and exploring key components related to that definition.

How can we live in a predetermined universe yet still be able to make novel choices and bring about alternative possibilities? This question highlights a longstanding area of debate in philosophy, psychology, and the sciences. Several scholars have long dismissed human agency as a mental illusion, arguing that such beliefs belong to "folk psychology" and are incompatible with a deterministic universe (Churchland, 1981, 1986; Sapolsky, 2023). These arguments claim that human actions are governed by predetermined physical laws and properties of our brains.

In contrast, scholars like psychologist Albert Bandura (e.g., Bandura, 1986, 2001) argue that humans are active agents who exercise control over their behaviors. This agency allows them to uniquely shape their lives and the environment around them. More specifically, Bandura (2001) does not reject the influence of biology or the way phenomena operate in the physical world. He rejects the view that biology or physical structures predetermine behavior:

> *Human evolution provides bodily structures and biological potentialities, not behavioral dictates. Psychosocial influences operate through these biological resources to fashion adaptive forms of behavior (p. 20).*

This perspective offers a more nuanced view that goes beyond simple *either/or* claims. For example, it challenges the idea that human behavior must be either entirely predetermined and aligned with scientific laws of the universe, or freely chosen and thereby making humans an anomalous and incompatible exception to those laws. Rather, Bandura's (2001) perspective is a *both/and* view. It recognizes both the possibility for the physical universe to operate under predetermined laws and for humans to still exercise some level of choice and control over their behaviors and actions in the world around them.

Philosopher Christian List provides a compelling argument in favor of this both/and perspective. More specifically, List (2023) asserts that accepting determinism at the physical level (i.e., "physical possibilities" governed by the laws of physics) does not require rejecting the idea that humans can exercise some level of choice and control over their actions and bring about new possibilities (i.e., "agentic possibilities," which have a degree of openness that we have some control over). According to List, physical possibilities and agential possibilities are compatible because they operate at different levels. An example might help clarify this compatible view.

Just as coding has a set of syntax rules that govern how the programming language operates ("physical possibilities"), human coders can exercise choice and creativity ("agential possibilities") in how they work with that programming language to create a vast array of programs and applications. The programming rules constrain but do not predetermine the possibilities for how coders develop new computer applications. The same can be said for a vast array of human endeavors, for instance:

- In the arts, sculptors exercise their agency by making creative choices within the constraints of a specific medium (e.g., clay), and poets often work within a formal structure (e.g., haiku).
- In business, employees exercise agency in how they approach tasks and provide goods and services to customers while adhering to constraints such as company practices, government regulations, and brand guidelines.
- In education, teachers exercise agency by designing unique lessons and tailoring their teaching methods to student needs within the constraints of curricular standards and school policies.

Our goal here is not to go too far down a philosophical rabbit hole but to provide a backdrop for realizing that human agency is always constrained. Those constraints, however, do not preclude people from intentionally making choices about when and how they will act in certain situations. Moreover, those choices can lead to new and meaningful changes in their lives and the world around them.

## What Is Creative Agency?

Scholars have conceptualized creative agency in various ways outside of psychology. Daniel X. Harris, director of the *Creative Agency Lab*, for instance, views creative agency from a socio-cultural perspective informed by posthumanist, new materialist, and affective theories (Harris, 2021), emphasizing an active, responsive, relational, and ethically engaged way of being in the world (Harris, 2023). Oliver Bown and Jon McCormack apply the concept to artificial life (i.e., non-human and computational systems), defining creative agency as "the degree to which [a system] is responsible for a creative output" (p. 255).

We define creative agency from the psychology of human creativity as:

*The intentional and self-directed capacity to envision and enact new and meaningful actions within the existing constraints of a particular context which can bring about changes in our lives and the world around us.*

This definition encompasses two key elements. First, the "creative" aspect addresses both novelty and meaningfulness, aligning with standard definitions of creativity (Plucker et al., 2004; Runco & Jaeger, 2012). Second, the "agentic" aspect emphasizes the intentionality of choices and the self-directed nature of actions, consistent with Bandura's (2001) conception of agentic action.

We also recognize that agentic action occurs within physical, sociocultural, and psychological constraints of a given context (Bandura, 2001; List, 2023). The central issue is not whether people can exercise creative agency, but rather what factors facilitate or impede it. Indeed, just because people have the capacity to exercise creative agency does not mean that they will.

Exercising creative agency is resource-intensive. As Baumeister (2008) has argued, exercising intentional choice and control over thoughts and actions requires expending psychological resources. Indeed, there is evidence that making choices and exercising control over one's thoughts and behaviors in one task *can* deplete performance on subsequent tasks (Baumeister et al., 1998; Muraven & Baumeister, 2000; Vohs et al., 2008). Although the assertion that exercising agency can deplete subsequent performance makes sense, recent work (Forestier et al., 2022; Hagger et al., 2016) has cautioned against describing this in simple or singular terms, such as "ego depletion."

Rather, researchers recommend taking a more nuanced, multifaceted, and dynamic view. Forestier and colleagues (2022) have, for instance, recommended describing the costs of exercising agency as "self-control fatigue," which can impair people's capacity, resources, and willingness to exert effort. They define self-control fatigue as "a temporary impaired effortful self-control act caused by an initial effortful self-control act that aimed to resolve a motivational conflict and decreased self-control resources, willingness and/or capacity" (p. 25).

Indeed, there are various personal factors, social pressures, and restrictions that can impede creative agency (Brehm, 1966). Consequently, people will likely exercise creative agency only when they believe the benefits outweigh the potential physical, psychological, and social costs. Put simply, creative self-beliefs matter when it comes to exercising creative agency.

## Creative Agency Beliefs

Understanding how people exercise creative agency requires examining the key decisions they encounter when considering creative action. In 2019, we introduced a model of CBAA (Karwowski & Beghetto, 2019). The CBAA model presented an empirically testable set of assertions derived from our own earlier work (Beghetto, 2006; Beghetto & Karwowski, 2017; Karwowski, 2011) as well as the contributions of others (e.g., Bandura, 1997; Tierney, 1997; Tierney & Farmer, 2002) on creativity and self-beliefs.

As this research program evolved, we recognized the need to expand this model to offer a more holistic, unified, and empirically testable theoretical account of creative agency. In our expanded model, creative agency is conceptualized as a series of interrelated decisions informed by four core self-beliefs:

- *Creative confidence*: Belief in one's ability to think and act creatively.
- *Creative centrality*: Belief that creativity is a central aspect of one's identity and personal values.
- *Creative risk-taking*: Belief that the benefits of engaging in creative actions outweigh potential costs or risks.
- *Creative self-regulation*: One's ability to use strategies and skills necessary for engaging with ill-defined creative tasks and overcoming challenges encountered along the path to creative solutions.

We also identified the need for a refined model to address lingering conceptual and methodological issues that have led to inconsistent findings across studies on these self-beliefs (Beghetto & Karwowski, 2017, 2019). Updating our model thus provides an opportunity to clarify and better align these concepts with the design of future studies, enhancing the field's understanding of how creative agency beliefs facilitate the translation of creative potential into action.

Our updated model of CBAA (building on Karwowski & Beghetto, 2019; explored fully in Section 6) identifies *four critical decisions* that shape whether and how individuals convert creative potential into creative action (see Figure 1):

1. **Can I do this creatively?** (Creative Confidence) This first decision is informed by people's creative confidence beliefs (fully described in Section 2). Creative confidence encompasses whether people believe they can think and act creatively. This belief is comprised of two interrelated sub-beliefs:
   - A general, trait-like belief in one's creative ability;
   - A specific, state-like confidence when facing creative challenges.
2. **Should I do this creatively?** (Creative Centrality) This decision examines whether people value creativity and view it as central to their identity (detailed in Section 3), including:

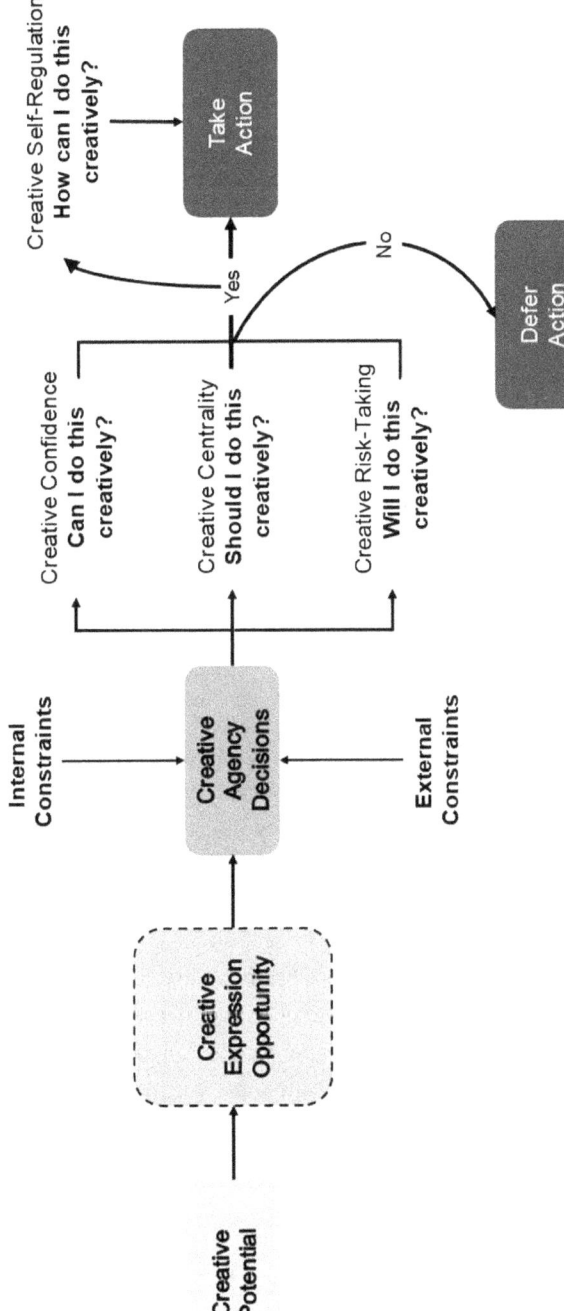

**Figure 1** Creative agentic decisions necessary for converting potential into action

- Whether people believe there is inherent value in being creative;
- How people assess the personal meaning of creative action;
- How these value judgments influence creative behavior;
- The role of sociocultural factors in shaping creative centrality beliefs.
3. **Will I do this creatively?** (Creative Risk-taking) This decision focuses on risk assessment (discussed in Section 4), specifically:
   - Weighing benefits against potential costs of creative action;
   - Willingness to embrace uncertainty;
   - Ability to face potential setbacks;
   - The role of prior experiences in risk-taking decisions;
   - The distinction between process-related and product-related risks;
   - The influence of contextual factors on risk assessment and decision-making.
4. **How will I do this creatively?** (Creative Self-regulation) This final decision involves implementation strategies (described in Section 5), including:
   - Using cognitive and behavioral strategies;
   - Managing thoughts, emotions, and actions;
   - Operating across three phases:
     - Forethought (goal setting, strategy planning);
     - Performance (monitoring progress, adjusting strategies);
     - Self-reflection (evaluating outcomes, learning for future tasks).

These four components work together as an integrated system within the CBAA model. While each component can be examined independently (and are individually discussed in Sections 2–5), they function interdependently to influence how individuals assess and engage in creative action. Their combined influence determines whether and how creative potential is converted into meaningful creative behavior, as detailed in Section 6.

As illustrated in Figure 1, these decisions become activated when we encounter situations requiring new thought and action. This activation occurs in situations such as when our previous approaches no longer serve us effectively, when we identify opportunities to create something new, or when existing solutions prove insufficient.

These decisions are shaped by both internal factors (such as our agency beliefs) and external factors (such as social and environmental contexts). To illustrate how these four decision points and their associated beliefs operate in practice, we present two contrasting scenarios. These scenarios demonstrate how creative agency beliefs can either enable or constrain creative action in real-world settings.

## Creative Agency Beliefs in Action: Two Scenarios

### Scenario 1: Diminished Creative Agency Beliefs

Consider Chris, a recently promoted shift manager at a popular restaurant. Chris notices persistent inefficiencies in the staffing scheduling process and recognizes an opportunity to creatively address this problem by introducing a new artificial intelligence (AI) scheduling tool.

However, Chris quickly experiences self-doubt (*Creative Confidence*). Despite recognizing that the AI tool is innovative, Chris questions their ability to successfully present and implement the idea. Although Chris has been generally confident in previous roles, the specific challenge of advocating for a technological change causes state-like uncertainty about their ability to convince senior management.

Chris also struggles to evaluate whether pursuing this creative solution aligns with their values and identity (*Creative Centrality*). While Chris generally values efficiency and innovation, they currently do not view creativity or proposing new ideas as central aspects of their professional identity, particularly within their new role. Additionally, the organizational culture seems to prioritize stability and adherence to established practices, further diminishing Chris's perception of creativity as a central or valued aspect of their new shift-manager identity.

Facing uncertainty about senior management's reaction, Chris carefully weighs the benefits against the potential personal and professional costs (*Creative Risk-Taking*). The potential advantages of improved efficiency seem promising, but Chris perceives significant risks associated with stepping outside traditional expectations and challenging established processes. Concerned about rejection, loss of credibility, or negative career consequences, Chris concludes that the risks outweigh possible rewards, further discouraging creative action.

Finally, Chris lacks clear strategies for managing uncertainty, emotions, and potential setbacks in moving forward with this creative solution (*Creative Self-Regulation*). Without established approaches for handling potential criticism, adapting their proposal to senior management expectations, or persisting in the face of initial resistance, Chris feels ill-equipped to successfully navigate the uncertainties of implementing this solution.

Taken together, these diminished agency beliefs (i.e., low creative confidence, limited creative centrality, heightened risk perception, and insufficient self-regulatory strategies) constrain Chris's decision-making, leading them ultimately to abandon the idea. Rather than taking creative action, Chris decides to maintain the inefficient but familiar scheduling process.

## Scenario 2: Robust Agency Beliefs

Now, let's imagine Dr. Jones, a college instructor teaching an introductory physics course designed for nonscience majors. Dr. Jones frequently hears students express frustration, complaining that the course content lacks relevance to their lives. Recognizing an opportunity for creative improvement, Dr. Jones develops a generative AI chatbot called *AppliedScience Bot* to help students explore practical connections between physics concepts and their everyday experiences.

Initially, Dr. Jones faces some internal doubts (*Creative Confidence*). While generally confident about their ability to introduce innovative teaching methods, recent faculty discussions about generative AI perpetuating scientific misconceptions cause some initial hesitation. However, Dr. Jones is confident that the *AppliedScience Bot* is different and believes it can help students see the relevance in what they are learning.

Dr. Jones also strongly believes that creativity and innovation in teaching are central to their professional identity (*Creative Centrality*). They view creative experimentation as a core value of effective instruction and perceive implementing *AppliedScience Bot* as aligned with their teaching philosophy and identity. This belief strengthens Dr. Jones's commitment to exploring new educational solutions despite the possibility of potential criticism.

In assessing risks, Dr. Jones acknowledges the concerns colleagues have raised about inaccuracies associated with generative AI but carefully weighs potential costs against the benefits of making physics more relevant to students (*Creative Risk-Taking*). Convinced that clearly communicating potential limitations to students can mitigate risks, Dr. Jones decides that the educational value of enhancing student engagement significantly outweighs potential drawbacks. Based on this assessment, Dr. Jones decides to embrace the uncertainty of implementing this instructional innovation.

Aware that resistance or criticism might arise, Dr. Jones proactively prepares strategies to manage potential obstacles (*Creative Self-Regulation*). When colleagues express skepticism midway through the semester, Dr. Jones is ready and provides a demonstration video illustrating *AppliedScience Bot's* effective use and positive student feedback describing how the chatbot increased engagement and relevance. Dr. Jones is able to effectively address colleagues' concerns and foster greater acceptance, prompting some colleagues to ask about adopting the chatbot in their courses.

Ultimately, Dr. Jones's robust agency beliefs (i.e., strong creative confidence, clear identification with creativity's central role in their teaching identity, willingness to embrace creative risks, and effective self-regulatory strategies) resulted in a successful creative outcome. Reflecting on this experience, Dr. Jones decides to pursue the development of an additional chatbot to support further student engagement and learning.

## Why Does Creative Agency Matter?

As we have discussed, when people exercise their creative agency, they can convert their creative potential into creative actions and achievements. Creative agency is, therefore, crucial at the individual and societal level. At the individual level, exercising creative agency can help us more productively navigate the uncertainties we face in everyday life. It can contribute to a sense of purpose, give our lives meaning, and promote well-being (Kaufman, 2023; Zielińska et al., 2023). It allows us to play a central role as the creative authors of our learning and lives – contributing to more positive and transformative futures for ourselves and others (Beghetto, 2023).

On a broader scale, exercising our agency plays a central role in the coevolution of individuals and cultures, simultaneously shaping our environment and influencing our development (Bandura, 2001). Exercising our creative agency can also contribute to societal progress and innovation. It helps in addressing complex societal issues and longstanding inequities, promoting economic growth, and bringing about positive social change (Sternberg & Karami, 2024).

In this way, developing healthy beliefs in our ability to exercise creative agency is not simply an additive luxury. Rather, it is necessary for healthy human flourishing and societal progress. Prior research on whether people believe they have choices and control over their own lives (Baumeister, 2008; Vohs & Schooler, 2008) suggests that people who lack such beliefs may exhibit decreased prosocial behavior and increased antisocial behavior, thereby hindering the motivation necessary for individual and societal progress.

Therefore, understanding creative agency and how it can be supported is a critically important goal for the social sciences, as agency plays a central role in individual and societal growth and survival. This issue takes on added importance in the age of GenAI, as such technological advancements present both positive possibilities for enhancing human agency (using GenAI to extend creative capabilities) and potential threats to people's willingness to exercise their agency (e.g., people deferring their creative thinking and actions to machines) (Faiella et al., 2025; Reich & Teeny, 2025).

## Overview of the Remaining Sections of This Element

In the remainder of this volume, we take a much closer and more detailed look at the theory and research on the four creative agency beliefs: creative confidence, creative centrality, creative risk-taking, and creative self-regulation. We discuss the early, contemporary, and future directions of theory and research on each of these beliefs.

We then offer theoretical assertions to guide researchers in exploring how these beliefs work together to convert creative potential into creative action (Section 6). Finally, we conclude with practical questions and strategies for cultivating creative agency (Section 7). Having introduced the nature and importance of creative agency, the remaining sections examine each component in detail, beginning with creative confidence in Section 2.

## 2 Creative Confidence: Can I Do This Creatively?

Creative confidence refers to the *belief in one's ability to think or act creatively across various performance domains* (Beghetto & Karwowski, 2023; Karwowski et al., 2019a). The psychological study of this construct emerged from creativity researchers' broader efforts to understand creative behavior and its underlying determinants.

Before discussing the historical roots and specific dimensions of this belief, it is important to clarify our use of the term *creative confidence.* While the concept of creative self-efficacy (CSE) is well-established and likely more familiar to many readers, we intentionally use the broader term *creative confidence* because it is grounded in recent theoretical and empirical developments within creativity research (e.g., Beghetto & Karwowski, 2017, 2019, 2023; Karwowski et al., 2019a, 2019b).

Our model of CBAA views creative confidence as encompassing CSE. Specifically, CSE represents the more state-like aspect of confidence beliefs related to specific creative tasks. The creative confidence construct provides a more nuanced framework, helping to resolve a longstanding misalignment in the literature that stemmed from the use of trait-like items in early CSE measures (e.g., "I am good at coming up with new ideas").

As Bandura (2006, 2012) cautioned, such items reflect general confidence rather than the more specific judgments characteristic of self-efficacy beliefs. This critical distinction and the broader concept of creative confidence will be explored in more detail later in this section. Clarifying this terminological shift is essential for understanding recent research developments in this area.

### Historical Roots

Interest in human creativity dates back to ancient civilizations (Glăveanu & Kaufman, 2019) and extends beyond the field of psychology. For instance, Alfred North Whitehead's philosophical work *Process and Reality* (1929) is often credited with popularizing the concept of creativity in scholarly discourse. Whitehead viewed creativity not as a psychological trait but as a metaphysical principle of novelty, emergence, and the continual process of becoming.

Within the psychology of creativity, Joy Paul Guilford's 1950 presidential address to the American Psychological Association is widely regarded as a pivotal moment, marking the beginning of systematic psychological research on human creativity. Importantly, we argue that Guilford's address also laid the foundation for research into creative confidence. Guilford explicitly emphasized the role of individual differences in creative expression, stating:

> *Whether or not the individual who has the requisite abilities will actually produce results of a creative nature will depend upon [ . . . ] motivational and temperamental traits* (Guilford, 1950, p. 444).

Guilford further discussed a "creative pattern" characteristic of individuals who make creative contributions. This pattern represents a set of enabling factors that facilitate the expression of creative behavior. Some of these factors are more deterministic (biology, environment), and others are more dynamic and personally determined. One of the personal determining factors that Guilford mentioned was *self-confidence* (Guilford, 1950, p. 444).

Although Guilford did not provide further elaboration on the role self-confidence plays in creative behavior, this recognition is reflected in much contemporary work on creative agency beliefs. As we noted in our introduction, contemporary work on creative agency beliefs examines the role those self-beliefs, such as creative confidence, play in converting creative potential into creative actions and achievements.

## Tracing Creative Confidence from Guilford to Bandura

Although shades of Guilford's assertions can be recognized in contemporary work on creative confidence beliefs, Albert Bandura's work has had the clearest and most direct influence on the development of related theory and research within the field of creativity studies. This is not too surprising given that Bandura's social cognitive theory (Bandura, 2001) provides extensive theoretical assertions grounded in empirical work, that explain how confidence beliefs influence agentic action.

Bandura asserted that no factor is more central to exercising personal agency than people's confidence in their ability to exercise control in their lives:

> *Among the mechanisms of personal agency, none is more central or pervasive than people's beliefs in their capability to exercise some measure of control over their own functioning and over environmental events* (Bandura, 2001, p. 10).

Bandura's emphasis on the central role of confidence beliefs in human agency provided a strong foundation for creativity researchers. This foundation helped researchers understand how creative confidence plays a role in determining whether individuals will take creative action and contribute to their own lives and the world around them.

Bandura specifically conceptualized this phenomenon not as "confidence" but as "perceived self-efficacy." Bandura (1997) defined self-efficacy as "beliefs in one's capabilities to organize and execute the courses of action required to produce given attainments" (Bandura, 1997, p. 3). It is thereby not surprising that creativity researchers borrowed this concept and adapted it to the field of creativity studies by calling it "creative self-efficacy." In what follows, we briefly trace how this borrowed and adapted concept of creative self-efficacy served as a starting point for work on creative agency beliefs and why we recommend incorporating it into the broader concept of creative confidence beliefs.

## Borrowing and Adapting the Concept of "Self-Efficacy"[1]

Early mentions of CSE appeared in the literature in the mid-1990s. Ford (1996) specifically referred to "capability beliefs," highlighting both self-confidence and creative self-image as elements within the "expectations and emotions that facilitate creative actions" (p. 1123, table 2). Plucker and Runco (1998) directly referenced "creative self-efficacy" in their call for creativity researchers to examine both task-specific and task-general aspects of creative production "during each creative moment" (p. 37).

Tierney (1997) and Tierney and Farmer (2002) were among the first to empirically examine the role of CSE in workplace creativity. They defined CSE as "the belief one can produce creative outcomes" (Tierney & Farmer, 2002, p. 1138) and developed brief, trait-like measures to assess it.

These scales typically employed items reflecting general creative confidence, such as "I feel that I am good at generating novel ideas" and "I have confidence in my ability to solve problems creatively" (Tierney, 1997; Tierney & Farmer, 2002), rated on Likert-type scales. Tierney and Farmer's (2002) influential study, demonstrating CSE as a significant predictor of creative performance, became highly cited and prompted further research.

Subsequent research often adopted this trait-like approach to measuring CSE. For instance, similar three-item scales were developed using trait-like self-assessments such as "I am good at coming up with new ideas" (Beghetto, 2006) or "I think I am creative" (Karwowski, 2011). In response to calls for

---

[1] This section is based on an updated and modified discussion of the emergence of creative self-efficacy in creativity studies (Beghetto, 2020).

more nuanced measures, later efforts included multi-item scales like the Short Scale of the Creative Self (SSCS), which expanded the number of items that assessed trait-like CSE and included items measuring creative centrality (Karwowski et al., 2018).

Research using these types of CSE measures expanded significantly, examining correlates, antecedents, mediating/moderating roles, and use across various domains (e.g., business, psychology, and education). A central concern has been the relationship between measured CSE and creative outcomes. Meta-analyses (Haase et al., 2018) indicate that such CSE measures account for approximately 8% to 20% of the variance in nonself-reported creative outcomes and a higher percentage (20% to 53%) in self-reported outcomes (Farmer & Tierney, 2017, p. 37).

However, the relationship between CSE and creative outcomes has yielded variable results, ranging from negligible to moderate effects (see Beghetto & Karwowski, 2017, for a discussion). While many factors contribute to this variability, one significant reason relates to how the concept of self-efficacy was borrowed and adapted, particularly regarding the conceptualization and measurement practices, which we discuss in the following section.

## The Benefits and Drawbacks of Conceptual Borrowing "Self-Efficacy"

Borrowing and adapting concepts from related fields comes with both strengths and limitations, some of which need to be addressed and corrected to ensure that research on creative agency beliefs contributes to knowledge and practice.

Conceptual borrowing from related (or distinct) fields can help to grow the conceptual foundations of a field (Ambrose, 2015). Indeed, work on CSE is one of the most widely discussed and studied of creative agentic beliefs. As of this writing, a simple Google Scholar search on "creative self-efficacy" returns more than 20,000 results. That said, conceptual borrowing also comes with its share of challenges and drawbacks (Berkovich, 2020), including distorted understandings, negative views of how the borrowed concept is used, and negative outside opinions of the work based on the borrowed concepts.

Consequently, scholars working with borrowed concepts often need to address and correct issues through retrofitting, renaming, and further specification of the measurement of these concepts to ensure that they are relevant and meaningful for research and practice (Ambrose, 2015; Berkovich, 2020). These retrospective "conceptual retractions" and corrections for borrowed concepts are both beneficial and necessary to promote better communication and indicate the positive growth of a field of study.

The same can be said of CSE. As we have discussed in detail elsewhere (Beghetto & Karwowski, 2017), initial scales used to measure CSE have resulted in some conceptual distortions of Bandura's concept of self-efficacy. These distortions diminish the accuracy and predictive power of CSE in relation to creative action. Therefore, some corrective action is required both in how the borrowed concept is described and measured.

## Limitations of Traditional CSE Measures

While initial CSE scales offer potentially valuable insights into creative ideational confidence, they often fail to capture the performance-based nature of self-efficacy beliefs that Bandura originally conceptualized. This stems from the tendency for these early scales to use global and trait-like items, rather than dynamic states that fluctuate depending on the specific task, context, and the individual's psychological state (Beghetto & Karwowski, 2017). This static approach obscures the nature of self-efficacy, which is influenced by various factors like prior experiences, feedback, and the perceived difficulty of the task.

Another limitation of global measures of CSE scales is that they use "indefinite" items that "do not specify the activities to be performed, at what level of attainment, the nature of the goals they are striving for, and what those 'valued outcomes' and 'challenges' are" (Bandura, 2012, p. 16). It is therefore not surprising that more global, trait-like CSE measures tend to yield weak to modest relationships with actual performance (Haase et al., 2018). These measures can also introduce potential confounds between self-efficacy beliefs about creative capabilities and the effects of those beliefs (Beghetto & Karwowski, 2017). As Bandura (2012) has cautioned:

> *These types of global measures of self-efficacy usually bear weak relation both to domain-related self-efficacy beliefs and to behavior ... Measures of general self-efficacy not only have problems of predictiveness. Most of them are seriously confounded as well. For the most part, they assess the cognitive, motivational, affective, decisional, and behavioral effects of self-efficacy rather than peoples' beliefs in their capabilities (pp. 17–18).*

Figure 2 contrasts the traditional, global approach with a CSE measure aligned with Bandura's (2006, 2012) recommendations, highlighting the difference in specificity.

As illustrated in Figure 2, the difference between traditional measures of CSE and a more conceptually aligned CSE measure is apparent. The global measures speak to more trait-like and general appraisals of creative confidence, whereas

Panel A

## Global Measures

### Creative Self-Efficacy (Beghetto, 2006)

*Items:*
I am good at coming up with new ideas
I have a lot of good ideas
I have a good imagination

Rating Scale:
1--------2--------3--------4--------5
Not true      Somewhat true      Very True

### Creative Self-Efficacy Items (Karwowski et al. 2011)

*Items:*
I know I can efficiently solve even complicated problems
I trust my creative abilities
My imagination and ingenuity distinguish me from my friends
Many times, I have proved that I can cope with difficult situations
I am sure I can deal with problems requiring creative thinking
I am good at proposing original solutions to problems

Rating Scale:
1--------2--------3--------4--------5
Definitely not    Sometimes    Definitely yes

Panel B

## Conceptually Aligned Measure

### Creative Self-Efficacy: Creative Idea Development Science

Please rate how certain you are that you can come up with, share, and develop a creative idea into a science project that others recognize as creative.

Rate your degree of confidence by recording a number from 0 to 100 using the scale given below:

0   10   20   30   40   50   60   70   80   90   100
Cannot                Moderately                    Highly
do it at all          can do                        certain
                                                    can do

|  | Confidence (0 – 100) |
|---|---|
| Come up with a creative idea in science class | ____ |
| Share my creative idea with only my teacher | ____ |
| Share my creative idea with the entire class | ____ |
| Develop my idea into a creative science project | ____ |
| Develop a project that peers and teachers think is creative | ____ |
| Develop a project that science fair judges think is creative | ____ |

**Figure 2** Difference between global and conceptually aligned measures

the more aligned measure focuses on confidence tailored to a particular domain of activity (e.g., idea development in science).

Moreover, the aligned measure assesses confidence in different types and levels of performance. Logically (and likely empirically), this measure would be a stronger predictor of a student's demonstrated ability to develop a creative idea into a creative science project that external audiences would recognize as creative.

Again, this is not to say one measure is necessarily better than the other. Instead, it highlights that creativity researchers should carefully consider what questions they seek to address when determining how to measure this creative agency belief. In some cases, researchers may decide to use one type over the other (e.g., use tailored measures when the question pertains to actual performance). In other cases, researchers may choose to use both types of measures (e.g., when attempting to understand how more trait-like measures work in conjunction with more tailored measures).

From a theoretical perspective, individuals with high general creative confidence (e.g., those who strongly endorse statements like "I can come up with creative solutions to problems") would likely demonstrate higher confidence in creative performance in specific activity domains (e.g., "I can come up with a creative solution to this type of interpersonal problem"). This contrasts with those who have lower general creative confidence. However, because specific knowledge and experience within domains play a role in actual creative performance (Baer, 2015), we expect that more tailored measures of creative confidence would be a more robust predictor of performance in specific spheres of creative activity (Bandura, 2012).

Empirical evidence supports this theoretical assertion. Karwowski et al. (2019a) demonstrated that global measures of creative confidence predict domain-specific creative confidence, which in turn more strongly predicts creative task performance than global measures alone. This hierarchical relationship highlights the advantage of combining broad, trait-like measures and tailored, domain- or task-specific measures to better understand the relationship between creative confidence and performance.

Our goal in discussing the limitations of borrowing the self-efficacy concept for creativity research does not negate the value of global CSE scales. Rather, it highlights the need for more precise conceptual and measurement approaches while acknowledging the contributions of existing measures.

As research on creative agency beliefs continues to develop, it is essential that researchers further specify how creative confidence is described and measured. Doing so will require corrections to how it is conceptually defined and measured. We discuss these corrections and recommendations next.

## Corrections and Recommendations

A key issue in creativity studies is that the borrowed concept of "self-efficacy" has been used to describe two distinct facets of creative confidence: trait-like creative confidence and state-like creative confidence. This approach is not aligned with Bandura's (2012) recommendations on clearly defining and measuring self-efficacy and potentially leads to a lack of clarity in understanding creative confidence within the field. Therefore, we have recommended (Beghetto & Karwowski, 2023; Karwowski et al., 2019a) that creativity researchers adopt the broader concept of *creative confidence* and clearly distinguish between its trait-like and state-like aspects.

**Trait-like Creative Confidence.** Trait-like creative confidence is a global belief that aligns with and incorporates existing measurement scales (described earlier). This is because it represents a more holistic judgment of one's confidence to perform creatively in general or within a particular domain (e.g., science, business, sports, education, and the arts).

Trait-like creative confidence is more aligned with a person's creative self-concept (Beghetto & Karwowski, 2017; see also Marsh et al., 2019). It reflects general feelings and relatively stable judgments about one's confidence to perform creatively. These judgments are based on the totality of past creative performances (e.g., "I am good at coming up with new ideas") and comparative judgments (e.g., "My imagination and ingenuity distinguishes me from my friends"). As can be seen from these examples, our and others' traditional measures fit nicely under this conceptual correction and therefore can still be used when studying creative agency beliefs.

This conceptual correction also allows creativity researchers to explore the nature of more global, trait-like beliefs – both on their own and in relation to more state-like beliefs. For example, Zandi and colleagues (Zandi et al., 2025) examined the stability of these beliefs. They found that trait-like creative confidence is generally stable in the short and moderate term, but it can change over the long term. Other researchers have examined the factors that influence these beliefs. Their findings show that creative confidence can be shaped by individual abilities (Lebuda et al., 2021), personality traits (Karwowski et al., 2013; Karwowski & Lebuda, 2017), and social influences (e.g., Karwowski et al., 2015).

Concerning measurement practices, we recommend that researchers use existing CSE scales or develop new ones when their goal is to understand the role of trait-like creative confidence. This includes examining how it contributes to a person's broader creative identity, how it interacts with other creative agency beliefs in shaping creative performance, or when addressing questions related to this more stable and holistic form of creative confidence.

We also recommend that creativity researchers clearly acknowledge the trait-like nature of these measures when describing their methods and findings. Doing so will help advance the field's knowledge and understanding of this important aspect of creative confidence.

**State-like Creative Confidence**. State-like creative confidence represents a more dynamic and performance-based judgment about one's ability to attain various creative goals within a domain of creative activity. In this way, state-like creative confidence is more aligned with a person's CSE (Beghetto, 2020; Beghetto & Karwowski, 2017). State-like creative confidence, much like self-efficacy (Bandura, 2001), is influenced by individual (psychological and physiological state, past performance), social (relatable models, social supports, social persuasion), and contextual factors (nature and ambiguity of the specific task).

As we have discussed, this is a more situationally dynamic creative confidence belief, which likely will be a more accurate predictor of within- and between-group differences in engagement, persistence, and performance on specific activities (Karwowski et al., 2019b). One way to think about state-like creative confidence is that it becomes activated when researchers ask people to report on different types of creative activities and when they encounter those activities.

Moreover, state-like creative confidence will likely fluctuate when people engage with ill-defined (divergent thinking) problems. Such tasks lack predetermined solutions or single answers, creating increased ambiguity. As Bandura (2012) noted, such ambiguity can challenge and potentially lower self-efficacy beliefs. Consequently, individuals' confidence may rise and fall dynamically throughout the problem-solving process as they generate, evaluate, and abandon ideas without clear external criteria for success. Capturing these fluctuations is important because it offers insights into how individuals navigate uncertainty and manage the ambiguity of ill-defined problems.

This dynamic becomes even more pronounced in information-rich contexts. The amount and nature of information available during problem-solving can influence confidence. Although access to resources like the internet, collaborators, or AI tools might help resolve ambiguity and enhance confidence compared to working with limited information (see Faiella et al., 2025), it can also introduce added complexity.

Individuals must sift through, evaluate, and integrate varied and conflicting information, which can influence confidence as they encounter challenges or breakthroughs. Therefore, documenting these real-time shifts in state-like creative confidence is essential for developing a deeper conceptual understanding of how individuals sustain effort and adapt their strategies while engaging with ambiguous creative challenges.

We recommend that creativity researchers continue to develop studies and measures of state-like creative confidence. This includes developing measures that are more aligned with Bandura's (2006, 2012) guidelines, like the example presented in Panel B of Figure 2. We also recommend building on Bandura's guidelines to advance theory and research on creative confidence beliefs.

Rather than simply borrowing the concept and measures of self-efficacy, we recommend developing original research and knowledge that address questions unique to creativity studies. This approach will help foster growth in the field (Ambrose, 2015; Berkovich, 2020). We encourage researchers to develop more dynamic measures that can be used in conjunction with existing trait-like and state-like measures, like those displayed in Figure 2. These new measures could also complement other relevant tools, like those assessing other creative agency beliefs, physiological and emotional states, and perceptions of social support and pressures.

State-like creative confidence can, for instance, be assessed through dynamic measures administered at three critical points: immediately before, during, and again following task engagement. This temporal approach captures the dynamic nature of creative confidence across the creative process (see also Section 5 on creative self-regulation).

Dynamic measures are central to micro-longitudinal designs (Beghetto & Karwowski, 2019), which examine whether and how state-like creative confidence beliefs change throughout creative task engagement. These designs involve developing brief, minimally intrusive measures taken at various points – initially, during, and after task engagement. Such measurements provide more nuanced insights into the nature of creative confidence.

Micro-longitudinal approaches offer several advantages for understanding creative confidence:

1. Revealing why individuals with similar state-like "creative profiles" may demonstrate different creative performance outcomes;
2. Capturing temporal dynamics of creative confidence;
3. Allowing for examination of within-person variations across different contexts and tasks; and
4. Including behavioral assessments[2] to provide a more complete understanding of whether and how self-beliefs support actual creative performance.

---

[2] We would like to thank an anynomous reviewer of an earlier version of this Element for the helpful suggestion to explicitly include behavioral assessments that compliment and extend self-reported beliefs in studies on creative agency.

This approach enables researchers to uncover subtle patterns of creative development that might otherwise go unnoticed (Beghetto & Karwowski, 2019). Its value lies in capturing the nuanced variations in creative confidence and in examining how confidence interacts with performance over time.

It also supports the view that creative confidence includes both trait-like and state-like elements. This allows researchers to observe how different aspects of confidence appear in real-world creative tasks. Finally, because there can be a disconnect between what people believe or value and how they actually perform, behavioral assessments can provide additional insight into the factors that influence people's decisions to express and act on their creative agency.

## Concluding Thoughts

This section has traced the conceptual evolution of creative confidence beliefs from early theoretical foundations through contemporary empirical approaches. We have discussed both the value and limitations of borrowed concepts while suggesting future directions for more precise measurement and conceptualization. These insights inform our discussion of creative centrality beliefs in Section 3, particularly regarding how creative confidence and centrality beliefs work in concert to shape creative agency.

## 3 Creative Centrality: Should I Do This Creatively?

Creative centrality beliefs are critical to our creative identity. Specifically, creative centrality refers to *beliefs about the value, merit, or worth of creativity in relation to one's broader sense of self* (Beghetto & Karwowski, 2023; Karwowski et al., 2019b). What we value is shaped by our individual and social experiences in the world and, over time, constitutes our unique personal identity (Hitlin, 2003). Values reflect our desired goals, which vary in importance and serve as guiding principles for making decisions and acting in and across settings (Hitlin, 2003; Morris, 1956; Schwartz, 1994).

A distinguishing factor between people who choose to exercise their creative agency and those who do not is whether they see creativity as central to their identity and their life (Dollinger et al., 2007; Helson, 1996). We further assert and have empirically demonstrated that these beliefs are central to people's decisions about exercising their creative agency. Specifically, even if they believe they can be creative in a situation, they tend not to take creative action unless they see value in doing so (Karwowski & Beghetto, 2019).

The development of creative identity (Beghetto, 2021a) can be thought of as progressing through several stages. It often begins with initial interest and enjoyment in creative activities (e.g., "I'm interested in creative writing"; "I like to write"). This interest may evolve to aspirational goal setting (e.g., "I want to become a novelist"). With sustained progress and continued engagement, the process can culminate in identity integration (e.g., "I am a writer").

This developmental path typically unfolds over many years and continues throughout life, adapting as personal goals and circumstances change. However, setbacks, such as repeated manuscript rejections, can indefinitely interrupt or halt this progression (Beghetto & Dilley, 2016).

## Creative Centrality

While the concept of creative centrality is generally understood, researchers vary somewhat in their specific definitions. Zielińska et al. (2024), for instance, define it as people viewing creativity as being vital to their self-perception and identity (including both personal and professional role identities; see also Huang et al., 2019). In contrast, Thomson and Jaque (2023) define it as whether people view the creative process as being essential for their personal meaning-making and well-being.

What is common to these different definitions of creative centrality is that they speak to the perceived value of creativity in people's lives. Moreover, empirical work has demonstrated that indicators of these two conceptualizations of creative centrality are significantly related (see Thomson & Jaque, 2023). Although there are nuances in how researchers have described the centrality of creativity, they all tend to agree that it serves as an essential aspect of how we view ourselves, our identity, goals, and actions (Dollinger et al., 2007; Karwowski et al., 2019b).

## Should I Do This Creatively?

Creative centrality beliefs influence whether people choose to be creative when presented with the opportunity to do so. When individuals face an opportunity for creative action, they implicitly or explicitly ask themselves, "Should I do this creatively?" This question is not necessarily about external obligation or a universally "correct" approach. Rather, it represents a critical decision point rooted in creative centrality (i.e., the personal value and importance an individual places on creativity as part of their identity).

Because values serve as guiding principles (Schwartz, 1994), this question reflects an internal decision: "Is acting creatively aligned with my core values and sense of self in this context?" It is a question of personal congruence and determines whether the individual will exercise their creative agency. Although creative centrality beliefs are essential to how people view themselves, they work in conjunction with creative confidence beliefs and other individual and socio-cultural factors when deciding whether to take creative action.

These assertions require further explanation and are briefly discussed in the sections that follow. A more elaborate discussion of the complex links between creative centrality, confidence, and the remaining elements of the creative agency puzzle is provided in Section 6, which offers a detailed overview of the CBAA model (see also Karwowski & Beghetto, 2019).

## The Relationship with Confidence Beliefs

Creative centrality beliefs have been conceptualized as more stable or trait-like than creative confidence beliefs (Beghetto & Karwowski, 2017). Therefore, they can be thought of as being "transsituational" (Schwartz, 1994), meaning they transcend specific situations (Hitlin, 2003). Indeed, if we view being creative as so central to who we are, then we would be more likely to exercise our creative agency in and across situations that afford us opportunities to demonstrate our creativity.

However, this does not mean that people who highly value creativity will choose to be creative in every situation. As Ford (1996) explained, simply valuing creativity is not enough. Other factors can override this belief when it comes to taking creative action. Before deciding to exercise their agency, people need to see an alignment among the situation, their self-beliefs, and their relevant knowledge and abilities.

Indeed, deciding whether to act creatively is influenced by creative confidence beliefs, along with individual and sociocultural constraints and affordances present in each situation (Glăveanu, 2013). For example, an engineer may value innovative design. However, if they are facing a tight deadline, believe their manager prefers to avoid risk, and feel unsure about applying a new technique, they may choose a more standard, routine approach instead.

Creative centrality beliefs and creative confidence beliefs work together to establish a threshold for creative action (Karwowski & Beghetto, 2019). When viewed through the lens of Expectancy × Value Theory (Eccles & Wigfield, 2002), people are most likely to exercise their creative agency when two conditions are met. They need to expect success (reflecting creative confidence) and value engaging creatively with the task. If either condition is missing, creative action becomes less likely. For example, if people do not believe they can be creative in a particular situation (regardless of the reason), they are unlikely to act creatively, even if they highly value creativity.

Conversely, even if people have confidence in performing a task creatively, they likely will not exercise their creative agency unless it aligns with their personal values (i.e., "Being creative is not important to me"). In this way, creative centrality beliefs moderate people's decisions to exercise their creative agency, even when they have confidence in their ability to perform creatively. Our empirical work has provided support for this assertion.

In a series of studies (Karwowski & Beghetto, 2019), we examined the role that creative confidence and creative centrality beliefs play in exercising creative agency (i.e., transforming creative potential into creative behavior). We found that although creative confidence beliefs mediated the link between creative potential and behavior, this link was not observed unless people also valued creativity above a certain threshold. These findings support our claim that for people to exercise their creative agency, they need to both believe they can act creatively (creative confidence beliefs) and believe they should (creative centrality beliefs).

## Individual and Socio-Cultural Factors

Beyond creative confidence beliefs, various individual and socio-cultural factors can influence people's decisions about exercising their creative agency on a project or task. Although valuing creativity represents a core aspect of our creative identity, people's decisions about whether they should take creative action do not occur in a vacuum.

At the individual level, certain facets of personal identity complement creative centrality beliefs and the exercise of creative agency. These include openness to experience (Karwowski et al., 2013), curiosity (Karwowski, 2012; Karwowski & Zielińska, 2024), and valuing individual differences (Anderson, 2024, Dollinger et al., 2017). Other facets of personal identity may conflict with valuing creativity and exercising agency, such as valuing conformity, tradition, and security (Anderson, 2024; Dollinger et al., 2017). The relative strength of these competing facets plays a role in whether a person chooses to act creatively when given the opportunity to do so.

At the sociocultural level, complementary and conflicting messages and pressures about what is valued in a particular situation or setting can also influence whether people decide to exercise their creative agency. Motivation researchers (Ames, 1992; Maehr & Midgley, 1991) and ecological psychologists (Schoggen, 1989) have long recognized the impact of both tacit and overt motivational messages and socio-psychological pressures in different environments. These factors shape people's behaviors, including their decisions about whether they should act creatively (Amabile et al., 1986).

If these motivational messages and behavioral pressures are highly salient and conflict with valuing creativity, then individuals who generally value creativity may still decide against exercising their creative agency in those situations or settings. This can happen when there is not sufficient support for creative action. Consequently, we assert that for people to decide they should exercise their creative agency in a given setting, one of two conditions likely needs to be met. Either their creative centrality beliefs must be more personally persuasive than the conflicting messages they receive, or the messages must be supportive of taking creative action.

These individual and social factors speak to the importance of people knowing when and when not to take creative risks, which involves assessing whether the benefits to themselves and others outweigh the potential costs. In other words, these factors influence people's decisions about whether they *will* take creative action, which is the focus of the next section. Taken together, these theoretical assertions outline our view on how creative centrality beliefs, creative confidence, and individual and socio-cultural factors influence people's decisions about acting creatively.

Although these assertions have a basis in theoretical and empirical work, much additional work is needed to test and refine them. For this work to continue to develop, it is important for creativity researchers to understand how to assess creative centrality beliefs and include those measures in their studies on creative agentic behavior.

## Studying Creative Centrality Beliefs

Historically, creativity researchers recognized the importance of valuing creativity (Guilford, 1950) and asserted that creative people view it as a core value (Barron, 1969; Dollinger et al., 2007; Helson, 1996). However, creativity researchers' interest in assessing whether personally valuing creativity impacts creative performance is a relatively new area of focus. Although this is an emerging area of research, there are notable examples of creativity researchers studying the relationship between valuing creativity and creative performance.

Given that creative centrality beliefs constitute part of one's personal identity, researchers have operationalized them as relatively stable and somewhat global. This is because our beliefs about the value of creativity are based on past experiences and socialization (Dollinger et al., 2017) in relation to one's broader sense of self (Beghetto & Karwowski, 2023). Consequently, researchers tend to use more general measures when studying creative centrality beliefs.

Dollinger et al. (2007), for instance, used an existing values survey (Schwartz Values Survey; Schwartz, 1992) to measure university students' value priorities. This survey includes an item asking participants to rate the importance of "Creativity (uniqueness, imagination)."

They also had participants complete a self-assessment of creative accomplishments (Hocevar's, 1979, Creative Behavior Inventory). A portion of the sample completed three scored creative products: a drawing product, a story product, and a photo essay. The creative centrality item was the best individual item predictor of self-reported creative accomplishments and a significant predictor of the composite rating for all creative products.

One of the most common ways creativity researchers assess creative centrality beliefs is through self-report items on the *Short Scale of the Creative Self* (SSCS, Karwowski et al., 2018). Five items (e.g., "I think I am a creative person," "My creativity is important for who I am") from the scale assess the domain-general and trait-like nature of creative centrality.

Empirical work based on the SSCS indicates that people's creative centrality beliefs tend to be relatively stable. While generally stable, this does not mean these beliefs cannot change over time or respond to interventions designed to help people recognize the value of creativity in their lives. Evidence suggests that these centrality beliefs tend to be stable in the short term but change as people age.

Karwowski (2016), for example, found that although these beliefs tend to be stable when measured in the short term, creative centrality beliefs grow from late adolescence to early adulthood and then decline in older adults. These results make sense, given that the centrality of creativity likely grows as people have more opportunities to exercise their creative agency during their transition to adulthood. Then, over time, the centrality of creativity may become more calibrated in later adulthood for people who do not view it as essential to their lives.

Regarding changes resulting from interventions, McVeigh et al. (2023) examined the impact of an intervention focused on teaching about creativity and the creative process in an undergraduate screenwriting course. They found that the intervention significantly improved participants' creative centrality beliefs (as assessed with the SSCS) and their creative performance. This finding makes sense, as the intervention likely helped students recognize the importance of creativity in relation to their screenwriting identity and goals. If participants initially lacked this connection, a course that clearly linked creativity to their chosen field would be expected to enhance their creative centrality beliefs.

We would therefore assert that although creative centrality beliefs are relatively stable, it is essential for researchers and practitioners to continue exploring the extent to which such beliefs vary and change because of life experiences and interventions. We would also recommend that additional work focus on how creative centrality beliefs vary across situations and tasks.

Given that prior research (Baer, 2015) demonstrated that different levels of creative achievement tend to be contingent on different domains, it is plausible that creative centrality beliefs also vary in relation to specific performance domains. Indeed, highly accomplished creative teachers likely value creativity in teaching because teaching is so central to their identity. Those creative teachers, however, may not value creativity in activities other than teaching.

Future research could explore whether and how creative centrality beliefs vary in and across performance domains by using a combination of existing measures domain-general items (e.g., SSCS) as well as items tailored to specific domains (Beghetto & Karwowski, 2023), such as *"Creativity is central to my identity as a [domain specific role]."*

## Concluding Thoughts

Valuing creativity and seeing it as central to an one's identity are key factors in the decision to take creative action. As discussed, creative centrality beliefs are essential to creative identity and work with creative confidence beliefs and supportive environments to influence creative behavior. Understanding these beliefs helps clarify how personal identity and sociocultural factors shape creative action across everyday life, education, the workplace, and broader society.

Consequently, it is important that creativity researchers continue to develop research programs that contribute to our understanding of the role creative centrality beliefs play in supporting creative action. Creativity researchers can, for instance, study the conditions that help teachers and students recognize the value of exercising their creative agency in schools and classrooms. This includes examining the individual and socio-environmental factors that support the development of teachers' and students' creative identities, and identifying the conditions underwhich they choose to exercise their creative agency. Additional research in organizations and everyday life is also needed.

For example, what role do organizational leaders and environmental conditions play in reinforcing the value of creativity and encouraging employees to approach their work more creatively (Beghetto & Karwowski, 2023)? In the context of everyday life, researchers can continue to explore how engaging in creative activities can promote meaning (Kaufman, 2023) and well-being (Putney et al., 2024). Indeed, deepening our understanding of creative centrality beliefs across various domains may help unlock people's collective creative potential in their learning, work, lives, and society.

Ultimately, recognizing the importance of creative centrality beliefs underscores the idea that creativity is not just about ability but also about personal identity. By helping people see creativity as central to who they are, we can expect them to be more likely to take the risks necessary for creative action, which is the focus of the next section.

## 4 Creative Risk-Taking: Will I Do This Creatively?

Creative risk-taking beliefs refer to *the willingness to think and act in new and meaningful ways when the perceived benefits to ourselves and others outweigh the potential costs* (Beghetto, 2019; Beghetto et al., 2021). Creativity researchers have long recognized that the willingness to take risks is necessary for creative action (Haefele, 1962; Kaufman, 2016). Creative action is risky because the outcomes of creative efforts are inherently uncertain (Beghetto, 2019; Getzels & Jackson, 1962).

Indeed, taking creative action often involves experiencing and working through setbacks and failures (Sternberg & Lubart, 1995; von Thienen et al., 2017). Moreover, because creative outcomes have emergent properties (Sawyer, 2012), it is difficult to predict the products, solutions, or outcomes of our creative endeavors. In fact, if the problem, process, and outcomes were well defined in advance, we wouldn't need to act creatively.

Creative action is only necessary when we face ill-defined problems or attempt to bring something new into the world without a clear path or predetermined solution. In such situations, we need to decide (Byrnes, 1998) that the benefits of engaging with uncertainty outweigh the potential costs and, if so, be willing to act on that decision (Breakwell, 2014). This is the very definition of what is meant by taking acceptable or *creative* risks.

### Conceptualizing and Studying Creative Risk-Taking

Despite extensive discussion in the creativity studies literature regarding the relationship between risk-taking and creative behavior, the field lacks a coherent framework for understanding this connection. Some researchers, for example, conceptualize risk as a predictor of creativity, whereas others view creativity as predicting risk-taking (Crepaldi et al., 2024).

These inconsistencies are also reflected in mixed empirical findings. Some studies (Beghetto et al., 2021; Charyton et al., 2013; Harada, 2020; Shen et al., 2018) have demonstrated links between indicators of creative risk-taking (e.g., willingness to take risks, risk tolerance, and risk-seeking) and creativity measures (e.g., creative activities and divergent thinking). Other research suggests more complex relationships. For instance, some studies found no significant correlation or only task- and domain-specific relationships between risk-taking and creativity (Jose, 1970; Pankove & Kogan, 1968; Tyagi et al., 2017).

In their systematic review of fifteen studies, Crepaldi and colleagues (2024) attribute these conflicting results to three key factors:

1. Inconsistent definitions of creativity and creative risk-taking;
2. Methodological variations in measurement approaches (e.g., self-report vs. behavioral tasks); and
3. Unaccounted for sociocultural influences.

These findings underscore the need for a more robust theoretical framework to conceptualize and study the relationship between creative risk-taking and creative behavior.

Our updated CBAA framework (detailed in Section 6) offers a systematic approach to understanding the relationship between creative risk-taking beliefs and creative behavior. It addresses the theoretical gaps identified by Crepaldi et al. (2024). Building on previous sections, the CBAA framework incorporates precise definitions of:

- *Creative risk-taking beliefs:* The willingness to act creatively when perceived benefits outweigh potential costs.
- *Creative agentic behavior:* The intentional and self-directed capacity to enact creative actions within contextual constraints.

In the sections that follow, we build on those definitions and describe empirically testable factors that inform people's beliefs and decisions to take creative risks (i.e., Will I do this creatively?). We also discuss theoretically aligned approaches for systematically investigating creative risk-taking within and across settings.

## Will I Do This Creatively?

Our CBAA model positions creative risk-taking as a pivotal belief in determining whether people *will* try to do something creatively. However, the relationship between creative risk-taking beliefs and creative behavior is more dynamic and multifaceted than a simple, direct link.

Like the creative confidence and centrality beliefs discussed in Sections 2 and 3, creative risk-taking beliefs demonstrate both stability and situational variability. This dual nature – combining both trait-like stability and state-like contextual responsiveness – aligns with other agentic beliefs in our framework. We posit that the more trait-like features of creative risk-taking are informed by prior experiences with creative risk-taking and related agentic beliefs (e.g., creative confidence and viewing creativity as central to one's identity).

Empirical evidence supports this assertion (Beghetto et al., 2021). Findings from the study ($N = 803$) demonstrated that a general (trait-like) creative risk-taking orientation moderates the relationship between creative confidence beliefs and creative behavior. Risk-taking was measured using a self-report scale, with items such as "I like doing new things, even if I'm not very good at them" and "I try to learn new things even if I might make mistakes." Creative confidence was measured using six global, trait-like items from the *Short Scale of the Creative Self* (Karwowski et al., 2018). Creative behavior was assessed with the *Creative Achievement Questionnaire* (Carson et al., 2005) and a modified version of the *Inventory of Creative Activities and Achievements* (Diedrich et al., 2018).

The findings indicate that even when people have high levels of general creative confidence, they also need to be willing to take creative risks for their confidence to translate into creative behavior. This finding aligns with our observations on creative centrality beliefs (discussed in Section 3), which moderate the relationship between creative confidence and creative behavior (Karwowski & Beghetto, 2019).

Based on these findings, we posit that three trait-like creative agency beliefs (confidence, centrality, and risk-taking) are necessary for converting creative potential into action. We further posit that domain- and task-specific agency beliefs may predict creative performance more accurately than global beliefs across different situations (Beghetto & Karwowski, 2017; Tyagi et al., 2017). These assertions underscore the need for a theoretical framework that incorporates global and domain-specific aspects of creative risk-taking.

The updated CBAA model addresses this need by providing an integrated framework encompassing multiple analysis levels. Specifically, the model identifies three key determinants of creative risk-taking decisions:

1. Prior experiences with creative risk-taking,
2. Global and situational creative risk appraisal, and
3. Context-specific influences.

The following sections examine each factor in detail, demonstrating how they influence creative risk-taking.

## Prior Experiences with Creative Risk-Taking

Theoretically speaking, prior experiences likely will have an impact on creative risk-taking. For example, if a person has experienced negative performance outcomes, particularly those involving shame and perceived inability to improve, their willingness to pursue similar creative aspirations likely diminishes (Beghetto, 2013; 2014). We therefore assert that prior experiences with creative risk-taking, particularly those with negative outcomes, can stifle the willingness to take future creative action (see also Beghetto & Dilley, 2016 and Section 5).

Although this assertion makes intuitive sense, understanding creative risk-taking more systematically requires examining actual prior experiences and testing how those experiences influence the willingness to take risks. Much research on creative risk-taking, including ours, has not sufficiently investigated prior experiences with risk-taking. Moreover, this research often neglects key aspects of those experiences, such as their frequency, domain, and emotional valence, and how these relate to future creative risks.

Consequently, more robust theoretical and methodological specifications are needed to examine how prior risk-taking experiences influence willingness to take creative action. In the following sections, we outline theoretical assertions related to prior risk-taking and propose methods for assessing these experiences.

Prior experiences may influence future risk-taking behavior through two primary mechanisms that operate in opposing directions. Positive experiences with creative risk-taking tend to increase the willingness to engage in future creative risks (Denrell, 2007). These experiences likely build confidence in one's risk-taking abilities and establish positive outcome expectations, creating a reinforcing cycle that supports continued creative risk-taking behavior.

In contrast, negative or limited experiences with creative risk-taking can have inhibitory effects, as negative experiences are often more salient than positive ones (Baumeister et al., 2001). Such experiences can reduce the willingness to engage in future creative risk-taking and heighten sensitivity to potential negative outcomes. This heightened sensitivity often generates risk-avoidant behaviors that can persist over time (Beghetto & Dilley, 2016).

This tendency toward risk aversion (Blair & Mumford, 2007) carries two important implications for understanding creative agency. First, most individuals require external support and encouragement to overcome their reluctance to engage in creative risk-taking (Dewett, 2006). Second, the willingness to take creative risks likely varies across domains (Baer, 2015), such as the arts, sciences, and business.

We encourage researchers to design studies examining the role that key features of past risk-taking experiences play in people's willingness to take creative risks on a given task, including:

- the frequency of prior creative risk-taking,
- past risk-taking experiences within specific domains or tasks, and
- the extent to which people judge their prior risk-taking experiences as positive, negative, or neutral.

### Assessing Prior Risk-Taking Experiences

Assessing prior risk-taking experiences should, at a minimum, account for the frequency, domain, or task and the emotional valence of those earlier experiences. To implement this approach, researchers can use various methods to capture these dimensions systematically.

For instance, studies might use quantitative items asking participants to rate the frequency of their past creative risk-taking in relevant domains (e.g., using scales ranging from "never" to "very often or always"). To assess domain or task specificity, participants could respond to checklists or open-ended questions identifying the areas in which they have previously taken creative risks. The subjective evaluation of these experiences could be measured using Likert-type scales that ask participants to rate the overall outcome of their past risks (e.g., from "very negative" to "very positive").

In addition, researchers could incorporate qualitative methods, such as brief written prompts inviting participants to describe a significant experience involving creative risk-taking. These prompts might encourage participants to explain the risks they took, the reasoning behind them (including perceived costs and benefits), the context of the experience, the outcome (positive, negative, or neutral), and how the experience influenced their subsequent willingness to take similar risks.

These qualitative responses can provide rich insight into the nuances of individuals' prior risk-taking experiences. This general approach can be adapted to fit various domains and tasks relevant to specific research questions (e.g., lesson planning or teaching, product development, artistic creation, research design, or other domain-specific creative endeavors).

Systematically assessing prior creative risk-taking in these ways can help researchers examine how often participants engage in such risks, the emotional valence they associate with those experiences, and contextual factors that may predict their willingness to take future domain- or task-specific creative risks.

### Global and Situational Creative Risk Assessments

When people decide whether to try to do something creatively, they can be thought of as performing a cost-benefit analysis. For example, they might weigh a potential benefit (e.g., If I share this unusual idea, it might help the group solve this problem) against a potential cost (e.g., People might also dismiss me or think I'm weird). As discussed, taking creative action requires a willingness to take creative risks, which is contingent on believing that the potential benefits to ourselves and others outweigh the possible costs. These risks, costs, and benefits vary across domains and situations.

In highly competitive environments, such as entrepreneurship, the situation often resembles a zero-sum game where one start-up succeeds while others fail. The risks these companies face include market rejection, failure to generate profit, and lacking distinctiveness or being easily copied by competitors. Avoiding risk entirely can result in not sufficiently differentiating from established businesses. A key task of successful entrepreneurs is to actively engage with risks so they can be reduced and managed. Consequently, successful entrepreneurs often possess broad business and start-up experience, ambitious goals, and clear yet adaptable business ideas (backed by long hours, personal investment, and strong communication) enabling them to tackle risk head-on and navigate external threats (Duchesneau & Gartner, 1990).

In less competitive domains or situations, the perceived risks might be lower, often centering on social acceptance or reputation. The potential benefits may also differ, including successful problem-solving, personal fulfillment, and contributing to others. This is not to say that less competitive domains necessarily diminish the experience or contribution of taking creative risks. Depending on the situation, creative contributions can range from personal and everyday to professional and more lasting (Kaufman & Beghetto, 2009).

We've already discussed how prior experiences with creative risk-taking and related creative agency beliefs (creative confidence and centrality) influence decisions to take creative risks. In addition, the CBAA model posits that a person's general orientation toward risk-taking *and* their situationally specific appraisals of the perceived costs and benefits will also play a key role in deciding whether people will try to do something creatively.

## Assessing Global Creative Risk-Taking

Global self-report measures are the most widely used by researchers to assess creative risk-taking (see Crepaldi et al., 2024). These measures can be used to evaluate people's general orientation toward creative risk-taking. Consider, for example, the scale we have used in our work (Beghetto et al., 2021) depicted in Figure 3.

The scale in Figure 3 uses items written to prompt respondents to engage in a cost-benefit analysis when assessing their global willingness to take creative

> **Intellectual Risk Taking (IRT)**
> (adapted from Beghetto et al. 2021)
>
> **Items:**
>
> I like doing new things when learning [benefit], even if I am not very good at them [cost].
>
> I share my ideas when learning [benefit], even if I am not sure they are correct [cost].
>
> I will try to do new things when learning [benefit], even if I am not sure how [cost].
>
> I try to find new ways of doing things when learning [benefit], even if they might not work out [cost].
>
> It try to learn new things when learning [benefit], even if I might make mistakes [cost].
>
> I ask questions when learning [benefit], even if other people will think I am not as smart as them [cost].
>
> **Scale Notes:**
> - 5-point Likert scale (1 = definitely not, 5 = definitely yes)
> - IRT scale score calculated by averaging responses across the above items

**Figure 3** General intellectual risk-taking scale.

**Note:** *benefit and cost have been added to illustrate how the items are written to induce a cost-benefit appraisal.*

risks in learning. It can also be used to assess specific learning domains (e.g., "...when learning [topic or subject area]").

The Intellectual Risk Taking (IRT) scale aligns with several dimensions of our definition of creative risk-taking beliefs, particularly the willingness to engage in new and meaningful behaviors within a learning context. However, global measures, like the IRT scale, can fall short when assessing a broader range of domain-specific tasks and contexts, thereby limiting their potential to serve as meaningful predictors of cost-benefit appraisals on specific creative tasks (e.g., developing a creative marketing campaign for a product, designing a creative experiment, and creatively performing a poem for a public audience).

Moreover, prior work on willingness to take creative risks often does not sufficiently distinguish between perceived risks involved in the creative process and the creative product or outcome. Making this distinction is important (Lubart, 2018; O'Quin & Besemer, 1999) because failing to do so can yield mixed results and inaccuracies in inferences about people's willingness to take creative risks.

When process and product are confounded and not sufficiently accounted for, it becomes impossible to answer key questions such as, "Do people lack the willingness to take creative risks because they view the process as being too costly to themselves or because they view the product as being too hazardous to themselves or others?" To enhance the consistency and accuracy of study results, we encourage researchers to distinguish between process-related and product-related factors when evaluating creative risk-taking.

Indeed, a person may be willing to take creative risks in generating ideas for a product (e.g., a wearable AI-powered assistant), but because they view the product as being potentially harmful (e.g., infringing on privacy rights), they decide not to launch the product. Separating these factors allows for more precise assessments of people's willingness to take creative risks.

Therefore, advancing research on creative risk-taking beliefs requires not only global measures but also situationally specific cost-benefit analyses – assessing risks involved in the creative process *and* the creative product or outcome.

## Assessing Situationally Specific Creative Risk-Taking

Researchers can assess creative risk-taking beliefs specific to a given situation or task to gain a more fine-grained understanding beyond global measures. This involves prompting individuals to engage in a cost-benefit analysis tailored to the immediate context, ideally just before they begin a creative task.

Such assessments should distinguish between the creative process and the creative product or outcome. For the process, the assessment can examine perceived personal costs (e.g., fear of criticism, time investment, and risk of rejection) and personal benefits (e.g., professional recognition, skill development, and opportunity for advancement) associated with engaging in the creative activity. Participants can be asked to identify and rate the importance of these perceived costs and benefits.

For the product, the assessment could focus on the perceived potential costs to oneself and others (e.g., negative impacts, ethical concerns, and societal disadvantages) and potential benefits to oneself and others (e.g., solving a problem, societal contribution, and user value) resulting from the potential creative outcome. Again, participants can identify and rate the significance of these factors.

Following this two-part cost-benefit analysis, researchers can then assess the individual's willingness to take creative risks in relation to their cost-benefit analysis. This willingness could be measured specifically for the perceived *process* and separately for the perceived *product*. Capturing willingness in this way can provide a deeper understanding of the kinds of considerations influencing people's decision to act creatively in a given context.

As this approach illustrates, researchers can add more situationally specific assessments of people's willingness to take creative risks. Collecting these types of data can help avoid confounds between process and product considerations and provide more nuanced insights compared to using global measures alone.

## Sociocultural and Contextual Factors

The final consideration for researchers interested in studying people's willingness to take creative risks pertains to examining and accounting for potential sociocultural and contextual influences. As Crepaldi et al. (2024) note in their review of research on creative risk-taking, this factor is often overlooked and results in inconsistent findings and an incomplete understanding of the role risk-taking plays in creative behaviors.

As with any creative agency belief, the willingness to take creative risks can vary across tasks, contexts, and cultures. These influences can be thought of as nested (cultures > contexts > tasks) and should be considered accordingly in the design of studies and analysis of data from such studies. At the broadest level of influence, researchers have noted that cultural influences and values may impact how people perceive risk and their willingness to engage in creative risks (Crepaldi et al., 2024).

Researchers have, for instance, discussed how views on creativity may be shaped by cultural differences between societies that emphasize individualism and those that place greater value on collectivism (Lubart & Sternberg, 1998; Niu & Kaufman, 2013; Tang et al., 2016). Whether and how societal values influence beliefs about creative risk-taking requires further empirical exploration. Consequently, research programs should examine how the willingness to take creative risks varies within and across cultural settings.

In terms of context, factors such as organizational culture, leadership styles, peer influence, and the availability of encouragement and support are also likely to influence people's willingness to take creative risks. Regarding the development of creative potential in young people, Anderson (2024) has demonstrated that contextual factors – such as the learning environment and instructional approaches – play a significant role in fostering young people's creative, agentic engagement.

In this way, whether creative risk-taking is valued and supported (rather than punished or suppressed) can significantly impact people's willingness to take creative risks and exercise their creative agency (Amabile, 1996; Edmondson, 1999; Zhou & George, 2001). This support includes encouragement to take small risks, which can help build experience and foster a greater willingness to take future risks (Beghetto, 2019).

Indeed, small wins can play a pivotal role in enabling people to continually reassess and adjust their willingness to take creative risks in new situations (Amabile & Kramer, 2011). Advancing research on creative risk-taking will require studies that examine these broader contextual influences.

Finally, different creative tasks also play a role in determining whether people are willing to engage with them creatively. High-stakes tasks (perceived cost of failure or loss > benefits of creative experimentation) will likely increase risk aversion (Kahneman & Tversky, 1979; Mumford & Gustafson, 1988). Even lower-stakes tasks can result in risk aversion, particularly when people experience constant monitoring and evaluative pressures to perform in expected ways (Amabile et al., 1996).

We assert that people are more likely to engage in creative efforts when they have sufficient creative confidence, recognize the value of completing the task creatively, and possess adequate prior knowledge and experience. Depending on the task, choosing not to approach it creatively can be a sound decision. For example, a student taking a final exam in high school algebra who spends time drawing anime characters instead of solving the test problems would be making a poor choice, as the potential hazards of this creative diversion outweigh its benefits.

Conversely, avoiding creative risks can also be a missed opportunity. Take, for instance, a musician who, fearing rejection, decides not to perform original music for a live audience or on social media. This choice may prevent them from sharing their creative work, connecting with audiences, and building a successful career in music.

Knowing when and when not to take creative risks (Kaufman & Beghetto, 2013), as well as how to regulate creative behaviors and emotions throughout task performance (Zielińska & Karwowski, 2022; Zielińska et al., 2023), is essential for developing and exercising creative agency. These self-regulatory decisions, which include understanding when and how to apply creativity effectively, are integral to achieving successful creative outcomes and fostering a willingness to take further creative risks. This topic is the focus of the next section.

## Concluding Thoughts

Exercising creative agency requires a willingness to take creative risks. As we've discussed, this is not a simple decision. Creative risk-taking is shaped by multiple factors, including past experiences, creative confidence, agency beliefs, situational risk assessments, and cultural and contextual influences.

While creative risk-taking is generally associated with enhanced creative performance, research findings on this relationship have been somewhat mixed (Crepaldi et al., 2024). To address these complexities, we need robust theoretical frameworks and research programs. Our CBAA model provides a comprehensive approach to understanding and studying creative risk-taking through the lens of agentic action.

Though initial results are promising, further research is needed to validate these findings across diverse populations, refine theoretical models, and develop interventions to support creative risk-taking. We encourage creativity researchers to expand on and test our theoretical assertions and recommendations, advancing our understanding of how creative risk-taking can be developed and sustained.

## 5 Creative Self-Regulation: How Will I Do This Creatively?

Creative agency supports individuals in deciding whether to engage in or avoid creative actions. Creativity involves generating novel and useful ideas but also requires persisting, exercising discipline, and managing thoughts, emotions, and behaviors throughout the process leading to the outcomes (see Sawyer, 2025). Thus, a complete theory of creative agency must conceptualize *creative self-regulation*.

Creative self-regulation focuses on whether people know how to use cognitive and behavioral strategies to regulate their thoughts, emotions, and actions before, during, and following creative action. It integrates cognitive, affective, and behavioral subprocesses that enable individuals to transform their creative potential into tangible outcomes by managing uncertainty, setbacks, and emotional challenges.

Creative self-regulation allows individuals to transition from perceived agency ("I know I can be creative, and it is important for me to behave creatively") to actual agency ("I know how to achieve creative goals"). This is why we consider self-regulation an essential element of creative agency. It enables us to take ownership of the creative process, make decisions, and persist in the face of obstacles by providing the tools necessary for managing these endeavors and exerting control over outcomes.

Creative behavior is an agentic action involving intentional and goal-directed behaviors. Self-regulation allows individuals to enact their creative agency by focusing on their goals, adapting to changing circumstances, and managing the emotional ups and downs of the creative process. Without self-regulation, individuals struggle to maintain momentum in creative tasks, become overwhelmed by uncertainty, or abandon projects when faced with setbacks.

This section traces the theoretical underpinnings of creative self-regulation. It explains its relationship with previously discussed creative agency beliefs (confidence, centrality, and risk-taking). Given that the question of "How can I do this creatively?" represents one of the most complex and multifaceted decisions of creative agency, this section provides a detailed treatment of this agentic decision. Furthermore, we briefly summarize the main findings from the growing number of empirical studies on creative self-regulation and characterize various self-regulation profiles people tend to demonstrate.

## Understanding Creative Self-Regulation

Self-regulation helps individuals manage and guide their activities to achieve specific goals (Karoly, 1993). It is generally understood as a set of cognitive, metacognitive, affective, and motivational steps that help individuals monitor and adjust their thoughts, emotions, and behaviors (Malanchini et al., 2019). Importantly, self-regulation is not only cognition-driven (i.e., related to the cognitive strategies applied); it also relies heavily on emotions and strategies for dealing with challenges.

Given this foundation, how should creative self-regulation be understood? In its broadest sense, creative self-regulation refers to consciously managing and adjusting cognitive and emotional processes required to achieve creative goals. This broad conceptualization naturally grounds creative self-regulation in general self-regulation theories (Bandura, 1997; Karoly, 1993) while also bringing a unique focus stemming from the challenges and dynamics of creativity as opposed to routine tasks.

While general self-regulation often focuses on controlling behavior to achieve a desired, well-defined goal (e.g., healthy eating or achieving a sport-related milestone), creative self-regulation requires flexibility in approach, tolerance for uncertainty, and the ability to revise strategies as new challenges emerge (Rubenstein et al., 2018, 2020). Like other forms of self-regulation, creative self-regulation involves goal setting, strategic planning, emotion regulation, monitoring progress, and revising approaches to meet creative objectives.

## Cold or Hot Self-Regulation: How Metacognition Differs from Self-Regulation

Creative thinking is often associated with spontaneous processes (Sawyer, 2012), such as mind-wandering (Baird et al., 2012; Christoff et al., 2016), intuition (Raidl & Lubart, 2001), or flashes of insight (Vallée-Tourangeau & March, 2020; Weiss et al., 2021). However, spontaneity represents only part of the story behind creativity.

It is well established that creativity requires not only idea generation but also idea selection (Bink & Marsh, 2000; Fürst et al., 2017). While exploration is undoubtedly important, so is systematic evaluation of various possibilities (Tromp, 2024). There is a scholarly consensus that executive mechanisms must supplement associative processes (Silvia, 2018) and that bottom-up (spontaneous) and top-down (controllable) processes interact in creative thought (Benedek & Jauk, 2019).

Even short-term creative thinking, like providing original uses for a brick, requires both spontaneity and control. Specifically, generating original responses in any divergent thinking task depends on recognizing and inhibiting obvious ideas that come to mind first, and such recognition and inhibition are examples of top-down executive mechanisms.

Recent research has focused on controllable aspects of cognition being analyzed within models of creative metacognition (Benedek & Lebuda, 2024; Lebuda & Benedek, 2023, 2025). Creative self-regulation, while related to metacognition (Kaufman & Beghetto, 2013), is broader in nature, as it also touches upon emotional, motivational, and behavioral mechanisms beyond pure cold cognition (Beghetto & Mangion, 2023; Kaplan, 2008). It applies to prolonged creative actions (Ivcevic & Nusbaum, 2017) rather than short-term creativity tasks, which mostly rely on creative metacognition. Managing creative actions requires both metacognition and the engagement of emotional and motivational mechanisms.

## How to Theorize Creative Self-Regulation?

Although creative self-regulation has only recently come to the creativity stage, several conceptual approaches have emerged in recent years. An initial framework for systematizing creative self-regulation (Ivcevic & Nusbaum, 2017) focuses on two interrelated processes. The first involves revising and re-strategizing goals and actions. The second emphasizes the role of mechanisms responsible for supporting and sustaining creativity.

Defining and revising goals is particularly important, given that creative tasks are often poorly defined and not entirely understood. This is precisely why creativity researchers underscore the role of problem-finding and defining goals before any attempts to solve them (Reiter-Palmon & Murugavel, 2018). Indeed, as illustrated by in-depth observations of creative actions across various domains (Glaveanu et al., 2013), creators often start with a vague idea of the goal they wish to attain and refine it while acting (Sawyer, 2025).

Such adjustments require balancing the exploration of various possible action directions while channeling efforts to turn an initial idea into an outcome. While revising and re-strategizing the activity, people must manage their goals, which are often ambiguous, particularly at the beginning of the process. This includes redefining and making the goal more precise and disengaging from goals that prove unfeasible.

Supporting and sustaining processes enable creators to persevere despite obstacles, uncertainties, and failures. Such persistence is driven by creative confidence and centrality (Beghetto & Dilley, 2016; Beghetto & Karwowski, 2017; Karwowski & Beghetto, 2019), but it also benefits from effective emotion management (Ivcevic & Hoffmann, 2019). Certain personality traits, most notably conscientiousness and its facet grit (Grohman et al., 2017; Rojas & Tyler, 2018), also play a role in this process.

The broad conceptual model proposed by Ivcevic and Nusbaum has recently been extended and operationalized in works by Aleksandra Zielińska and her colleagues (Zielińska et al., 2022, 2025a). Specifically, Zielińska and colleagues built a theoretical bridge between Ivcevic and Nusbaum's theorizing and self-regulated learning (SRL) models proposed in educational psychology (see Rubenstein et al., 2018, for applications to the creativity literature). This research program has proved fruitful by delivering new findings related to creative self-regulation, which are summarized in the next section.

### The Self-Regulated Learning Model in Creative Self-Regulation

As illustrated by Rubenstein and her colleagues (2018), Zimmerman's (1990, 2000) SRL model provides a helpful framework for understanding creative self-regulation and, more broadly, creative action. The SRL model categorizes regulatory processes into three often overlapping phases: forethought, performance, and self-reflection.

When applying these phases to creative action, we can see that during the forethought phase, individuals define, redefine, and set their creative goals, as well as consider strategies to navigate potential challenges. In the performance phase, people engage with the task while regulating their cognitive and emotional resources. Finally, the self-reflection phase involves evaluating the results of the creative endeavor, drawing insights from the experience, and considering how to improve future performance. This cyclical model captures the dynamic nature of creative work, where constant adaptation and revision are key.

### Phases of SRL

Previous studies have demonstrated that creative activity, both short-term laboratory tasks (Callan et al., 2021) and longer-term projects (Zielińska et al., 2024, 2025b), progresses through phases of forethought, performance, and self-reflection. In the preparatory phase (forethought), people define their goals and form initial plans for achieving them.

Creative confidence and prior experience within the domain help make these goals realistic and attainable. In the performance phase, creative action occurs, requiring not only engagement in the activity but also the use of cognitive strategies to manage the task, monitor the effectiveness of these strategies, and regulate their application. In the final phase of self-reflection, individuals assess the outcomes and consider the strengths and weaknesses of their approach. Each phase, particularly performance and self-reflection, is accompanied by emotional reactions.

Based on this phased approach, Zielińska and her colleagues (Zielińska et al., 2022, 2025a) developed a more detailed model of creative self-regulation that identifies seven regulatory mechanisms situated within the forethought, performance, and self-reflection phases. These mechanisms were further operationalized as a self-report scale that can be applied retrospectively by referring to previous actions and "online" during the activity itself.

In the forethought phase, Zielińska's and colleagues' model identifies a vital role played by two mechanisms: obstacle expectations and uncertainty acceptance. Obstacle expectation refers to the creator's ability to anticipate difficulties during the creative process. Awareness and expectation of what could be challenging are prerequisites for dealing effectively with such obstacles.

The second strategy, uncertainty acceptance, relates to the tolerance of ambiguity and unpredictability inherent in the creative process. People who understand and accept that they do not have all steps and subgoals predefined are more likely to react flexibly and adapt to various circumstances during the process.

The performance phase focuses on three self-regulatory mechanisms: the adjusting approach, managing and reframing goals, and emotion regulation. The adjusting approach refers to the flexibility and readiness to revise strategies when faced with challenges. Managing and reframing goals allows people to make their objectives more specific and attainable or shift the direction of action accordingly. Emotion regulation enables individuals to deal with frustration or apathy and to stay motivated.

Finally, the self-reflection phase involves two specific strategies and associated mechanisms. The first, the improving approach, involves reflecting on what could be done better or differently in future creative tasks. The second, readiness for sharing, describes the willingness to present one's creative work to others. These mechanisms represent a first step toward a comprehensive framework for understanding how individuals regulate their creative processes and offer a foundation for assessing creative self-regulation in different contexts.

## Measuring Creative Self-Regulation Tendencies

A method inspired by this seven-factor model, the *Creative Self-Regulation Questionnaire* (Zielińska et al., 2022), has not only been found to be valid and reliable but also instrumental in generating several findings that enrich our understanding of correlates, antecedents, and consequences of differences in creative self-regulation.

Results from an extensive research program – including in-depth qualitative interviews, large-scale cross-sectional and longitudinal studies in school settings, daily diary studies, experiments, and interventions – can be categorized into ten broad spheres:

1. Testing domain-specificity vs. generality of creative self-regulation,
2. Exploring self-regulation as a factor that makes creative activity effective – that is, allows it to more smoothly translate into creative achievement,
3. Testing the broader role of creative self-regulation understood as an individual difference variable (trait-like) for creative activity and achievement,
4. Examining the links and hypothetically causal mechanisms between creative self-regulation and other creative agency factors: confidence and centrality,
5. Showing the role of stable personality factors for creative self-regulation,
6. Testing the role of creative self-regulation for future creative activities and engagement,
7. Demonstrating the possibilities of experimentally inducing creative self-regulation through simple prompts and its effects on creative outcomes,
8. Providing evidence for the role of creative self-regulation alongside other agency factors in long-term real-life tasks,
9. Illustrating the potential of creative self-regulation interventions to stimulate other agency factors and creative outcomes, and
10. Establishing various creative self-regulation types or profiles that people might represent.

In the remainder of this section, we discuss key findings related to each of these ten aspects.

## An Empirical Decalogue of Research on Creative Self-Regulation

**1. *Creative Self-Regulation Is (Mostly) Domain-General.*** Creative self-regulation appears to be largely domain-general, meaning that various creative domains rely on similar structures and self-regulation mechanisms. However, different domains may vary in the intensity of self-regulation mechanisms needed to ensure creative achievement.

Measurement invariance analyses of the Creative Self-Regulation Questionnaire (Zielińska et al., 2025a) across three broad creative superdomains – arts, science, and everyday creativity – have shown that the structure of creative self-regulation is virtually the same across domains.

This finding indicates that measuring self-regulatory mechanisms across different domains is possible and allows for valid comparisons, as required by measurement invariance methodology. More importantly, it suggests that the ways people self-regulate during creative activity are essentially universal, regardless of the domain.

However, this does not rule out differences in the intensity of specific self-regulatory mechanisms involved in creative actions within different domains. On the contrary, an extensive study (Zielińska et al., 2025a) found that creative activity within science relied more heavily on nearly all self-regulatory mechanisms compared to those in the arts or everyday settings. The differences between the arts and everyday creativity were smaller and more nuanced.

While these findings do not preclude the possibility of additional, domain-specific self-regulatory strategies, they emphasize the foundational and broadly applicable role of the seven mechanisms outlined in Zielińska and her colleagues' model.

**2. *Self-Regulation Makes Activity Effective.*** The second finding highlights that self-regulation moderates the relationship between creative activity and achievement. While this relationship is generally positive and robust (e.g., Lebuda et al., 2021), recent research (Zielińska et al., 2023) shows that self-regulation plays a distinct role in translating creative activity into achievement. Specifically, the link between activity and achievement was stronger among individuals who effectively self-regulate compared to those who struggle with self-regulation.

Thus, although creative activity is essential for creative achievement, not all forms of activity are equally effective. Self-regulation enhances the creative process, increasing the likelihood of producing creative outcomes. These findings further support the idea that creative self-regulation is a key component of creative agency, providing the "how to create" knowledge and skills needed for success.

**3. *Self-Regulation Drives (and Is Driven by) Activity.*** The third empirical observation shows that creative self-regulation is positively associated with creative activity. This relationship has been demonstrated in studies on adolescents (Zielińska et al., 2022), adults engaged in various domains (Zielińska et al., 2025a), and creative professionals (Ivcevic et al., 2024). Although most of the studies rely on correlational designs, the nature of these links appears to be reciprocal.

This reciprocal relationship manifests in two ways. First, individuals who have experienced success in prior creative endeavors are more likely to develop self-regulation skills. These successes reinforce the belief that effort and regulation lead to positive outcomes, motivating continued growth and the use of self-regulatory strategies.

Observations of how creative professionals work (Glaveanu et al., 2013; Sawyer, 2025) typically portray them, contrary to popular myths (Benedek et al., 2021), as well-organized and self-disciplined, relying on specific, often idiosyncratic strategies they have developed and refined through practice. In this way, prior creative activity provides the foundation for building and sustaining creative self-regulation.

Second, creative self-regulation also predicts creative achievement. Research by Zielińska and colleagues (2023) demonstrated that individuals who use effective self-regulation strategies are more likely to produce high-quality creative work and succeed in creative fields. This finding is supported by various studies showing that using self-regulation strategies predicts performance in different creativity tasks.

For instance, Mawang et al. (2020) asked music students to complete a creative composition task. They found that higher levels of musical creativity in the compositions, as rated by expert judges, were associated with the use of self-regulatory strategies such as organization, elaboration, and critical thinking.

In another study, Jankowska et al. (2018), had participants complete a drawing creativity test while wearing eye-tracking glasses and providing spontaneous think-aloud comments. Those who scored the highest on the test took a distinctive approach: not only did they explore many possible solutions, but they also worked strategically, exercising continuous control over their process through planning, self-reporting, correcting, and elaborating.

Interestingly, self-regulatory skills can be learned through observation. Students who watched videos of peers engaging in creative design tasks – while simultaneously commenting on the process, such as explaining how participants explored the task, addressed problems, tried different solutions, and selected or combined ideas – produced more creative designs afterward compared to students who received instruction on how to do so (Groenendijk et al., 2013).

In sum, there is convincing evidence for a bidirectional relationship: activity drives self-regulation, while self-regulation enhances the effectiveness of activity and supports the transfer of effort into creative achievement.

**4. *Confidence and Self-Regulation Are Necessary for Creative Performance.*** Not only are there systematic and positive links between creative self-regulation and activity or achievement, but there is also convincing evidence for treating agency-related factors as "a must-have" for effective performance.

Consider a recent study (Zielińska et al., 2024), which examined teachers' creativity alongside their creative confidence and self-regulation. This study found that creative self-regulation mediates the relationship between creative confidence and creative performance.

Higher creative confidence was positively associated with creative self-regulation (as discussed in the following) and further enhanced teachers' creativity in their professional tasks. Notably, this study demonstrated that both confidence and self-regulation were necessary for strong creative performance.

In other words, creative outcomes were highly unlikely when either confidence or self-regulation was lacking. Although strong confidence or well-developed self-regulatory skills do not ensure creative achievement, their absence virtually guarantees creative failure.

**5. *Creative Self-Regulation Stems from Confidence. Creative Self-Regulation Builds Confidence.*** Another consistent finding across multiple studies (Zielińska et al., 2022, 2024, 2025a) is the relationship between creative self-regulation and creative confidence. Across these studies, the associations between these agentic beliefs were consistently positive and typically moderate in strength. But what are the mechanisms behind these associations?

According to classic social cognitive theory (Bandura, 1997), self-efficacy plays a causal role in shaping self-regulation. Applied to creativity, this suggests that creative confidence should likewise play a causal role in the development of creative self-regulation. Why might that be? There are at least three plausible mechanisms.

The first pertains to experience and success. Creatively confident individuals tend to have more mastery experiences (past creative successes), which serve as the foundation for developing creative self-regulation. This aligns with our earlier discussion of the reciprocal relationship between creativity activity (or achievement) and self-regulation. In short, creative confidence often grows out of experiencing success with creative endeavors. Through these experiences, people learn what works and what does not, making creative self-regulation a natural byproduct of creative confidence.

The second mechanism pertains to the nature of the goals that more creatively confident people formulate. Creative confidence is positively associated with more ambitious and far-reaching goals, which require more complex planning and strategies to navigate the creative process effectively. The nature of these goals likely drives creatively confident individuals to approach challenges differently and apply a broader range of strategies.

The third mechanism explains how more creatively confident individuals, due to their experience and ambitious goals, also possess a greater repertoire of strategies and are more open to experimenting with them. They tend to be less rigid and more adaptable, often having a "plan B" when initial approaches fail. However, there is also evidence suggesting that this posited causal link can operate in the other direction: self-regulation can strengthen creative confidence.

Consider an intervention study (Zielińska & Karwowski, under review) in which students' self-regulation was either activated (experimental group) or not (control group) during a three-week creative writing study. The activation of self-regulation translated into increased creative confidence. When students were given simple prompts to anticipate and address potential challenges, they felt more confident and creative in handling the task. Thus, the relationship between creative confidence and self-regulation is reciprocal, with each reinforcing the other.

**6. *Creative Self-Regulation Is Not Just an Epiphenomenon of Personality or Beliefs about Creativity.*** Personality traits are important for creative self-regulation, but their role should not be overstated. Research shows (Lebuda et al., 2021) that individuals high in traits such as openness to experience, conscientiousness, and emotional stability (i.e., low in neuroticism) are more likely to engage in effective self-regulation strategies during creative tasks.

Openness to experience is particularly linked to greater creativity, as individuals high in this trait tend to be more curious, imaginative, and open to new ideas. These qualities enable them to explore novel approaches to problems, tolerate uncertainty, and regulate their emotional responses to setbacks.

Conscientiousness, by contrast, is associated with greater persistence and goal-directed behavior, making it important for regulating effort in long-term creative projects. While creativity often requires the flexibility to explore new possibilities, it also demands discipline and self-control to refine and implement ideas. Individuals high in conscientiousness are particularly skilled in these areas, which supports persistent and effective engagement with creative work.

Emotional stability (or low neuroticism) supports the emotional regulation aspect of creativity. Those who are more emotionally stable can cope more effectively with the frustrations and uncertainties of creative work, allowing them to persevere where others might give up.

Yet, studies show that the links between personality factors and creative self-regulation are typically modest in strength (Zielińska et al., 2022, 2025a). While specific traits might play a more substantial role in specific strategies – such as openness for uncertainty acceptance or emotional stability for managing emotions – creative self-regulation should not be reduced to a combination of personality traits.

This assertion is supported by findings that creative self-regulation explains a unique portion of the variance in creative activity and achievement, even when personality factors are statistically controlled in multivariate models (Ivcevic et al., 2024; Zielińska et al., 2025a).

Beyond personality, another important correlate (and theoretically, an antecedent) of creative self-regulation is an individual's creative mindset, which refers to their belief about whether creativity is a fixed trait or a malleable skill that can develop over time (Karwowski, 2014; Karwowski et al., 2019c). Research shows (Zielińska et al., 2022, 2025a) that individuals who believe that creativity can improve through effort and practice (a growth mindset) are more likely to activate and use self-regulatory behaviors relevant to their creative performance.

A growth mindset fosters resilience in the face of setbacks, encouraging individuals to view obstacles as opportunities for learning rather than as indicators of failure. This mindset is crucial for self-regulation, as it helps individuals maintain motivation, adjust their strategies, and persist in their creative efforts.

**7. Self-Regulation Prompts Make People More Creative.** Research on creative self-regulation has increasingly focused on identifying causal links, such as how self-regulation influences creative outcomes through experimental designs. A recent experiment by Zielińska et al. (2025b) tested the effectiveness of brief self-regulation prompts in enhancing creative performance.

Participants were asked to complete tasks involving logo design, short story writing, or greeting card creation. Half received prompts encouraging self-regulation strategies. Those who received the prompts produced more creative outcomes than participants in the control group. These results suggest that even simple interventions can enhance creative performance by promoting strategic and controlled task engagement.

Moreover, the study demonstrated that the effect of the prompts was fully mediated by participants' engagement (measured by the time spent on the task) and their positive active emotions during the activity. In other words, self-regulatory prompts primarily influenced emotional (positive active emotions) and motivational (task engagement) aspects of the creative process, rather than only cognitive or metacognitive effects.

**8. Stimulating Creative Self-Regulation Strengthens Creativity Outside the Laboratory.** Interventions centered on self-regulation and implementation intentions build creative confidence, translate into various creative activities, and enhance creative outcomes. As demonstrated by Zielińska and Karwowski (in press a), students who received self-regulation prompts during a three-week creative writing project reported higher creative confidence and greater engagement in creative activities compared to the control group.

In addition, their stories were assessed as significantly more creative by independent judges who were blind to the experimental conditions. The positive effects of self-regulatory prompts were particularly evident in the early stages of the creative process, helping students to organize their approach and lay a stronger foundation for subsequent steps of the process.

**9. There Are (at least) Three Distinct Types of Self-Regulators.** Creative self-regulation is a process, yet individuals tend to have particular preferences regarding how they manage creative tasks. As such, creative self-regulation can be analyzed as an individual difference variable that varies across and within individuals.

A mixed-method study (Zielińska et al., 2024) identified three distinct profiles (or types) of people with different creative self-regulation styles. The three types are summarized in Table 1.

Importantly, these types are not necessarily fixed. Rather, they reflect how individuals regulate their creative processes, anticipate challenges, and adjust their actions to produce creative outcomes (Anderson, 2025).

**10.** *Creative Self-Regulation Brings Hope for Future Creativity.* Effective creative self-regulation is not only associated with creative activity and achievement (in what appears to be a reciprocal relationship), but it also increases individual's eagerness to pursue future creative endeavors.

At least three distinct findings support this hopeful outlook. First, in a correlational study by Zielińska and colleagues (Zielińska et al., 2025a), participants reported on their anticipated future engagement and creative achievement. Multivariate models demonstrated that certain self-regulation factors – most consistently emotion regulation and readiness for sharing – were positively associated with expected future creativity, even after controlling for personality traits, creative mindsets, and the other agency factors (e.g., confidence and centrality).

Second, findings from Zielińska and Karwowski (in press a) showed that participants who received self-regulatory prompts wrote more creative stories. One month later, they were also more likely to believe they would publish a novel someday, compared to participants in the control group or those who did not participate in the intervention.

Third, a study conducted by Zielińska & Karwowski (2023) examined "possibility thinking" related to future creative endeavors. Participants imagined themselves as authors who published a novel and described some details of this imagined book. They then rated the likelihood of actually writing such a book and responded to the Creative Self-Regulation Questionnaire with respect to this imagined task.

Perceived likelihood was positively associated with openness, creative confidence, and creative self-regulation, particularly in areas such as managing goals, emotion regulation, and readiness for sharing. Notably, individuals with low creative self-regulation were far less convinced that they could write novel someday.

Similar to the mixed-method study on teachers (Zielińska et al., 2024), three types of "creative self-regulators" emerged. Participants who envisioned their future actions in terms of a "dysregulated approach" were significantly less creatively confident and perceived their chances of writing a book as much lower than those who adopted a "plan-execute approach" or "draft-revise approach."

**Table 1** Creative self-regulation types

| Type | Definition & characteristics | Example | Support techniques & strategies |
|---|---|---|---|
| **Dysregulated Type:** Struggling with Control | Difficulty managing creative processes. Overwhelmed by complexity; struggles with planning, monitoring, and adjusting actions. Anticipates obstacles but fails to devise solutions, leading to paralysis and negative emotions. Reactive rather than proactive, often abandoning projects. Low-quality output. | A teacher envisions challenges in designing a new curriculum module but becomes overwhelmed and indecisive, failing to complete multiple started ideas. | **Structure and Guidance:** Clear frameworks, deadlines, and scaffolding.<br>**Strategy Training:** Techniques for managing frustration and uncertainty (e.g., cognitive reframing, time management).<br>**Chunking:** Breaking down tasks into smaller, manageable steps with frequent check-ins.<br>**Process over Perfection:** Encouraging a focus on progress rather than flawless outcomes.<br>**Incremental Feedback:** Providing feedback on small steps rather than waiting for project completion.<br>**Encourage Flexibility:** Exploring new ideas, creative risks, and iterative processes. |
| **Plan-and-Execute Type:** The | Highly structured, goal-oriented approach. Excels at setting objectives and following plans. | A teacher meticulously plans and adheres to | |

Table 1 (cont.)

| Type | Definition & characteristics | Example | Support techniques & strategies |
|---|---|---|---|
| Methodical Creators | Efficient, organized, and disciplined. Less likely to revise work once initial goals are met. High creativity when tasks align with the initial plan. | a timeline for designing a project-based learning module, considering it complete once initial objectives are met without exploring alternative ideas. | **Value of Revision:** Highlighting the benefits of revisiting and refining work.<br>**Opportunities for Experimentation:** Introducing scenarios that encourage deviation from the plan (e.g., design sprints, rapid prototyping).<br>**Collaborative Feedback:** Pairing with individuals who excel at risk-taking and improvisation. |
| **Draft-and-Revise**<br>**Type:** The Flexible Iterators | Dynamic and adaptive approach. Comfortable with uncertainty and expects obstacles. Open to multiple revisions, viewing them as opportunities for improvement. | A teacher developing an interdisciplinary project continually refines their approach, testing | **Reflection on Collaboration:** Encouraging reflection on how collaboration and feedback can enhance their approach.<br>**Guided Deadlines:** Providing structured timelines to avoid overworking or over-refining.<br>**Balance Iteration and Completion:** Encouraging a balance between refining and finalizing. |

Persistent, experimental, and comfortable with risk-taking. May be slower to declare a project finished, often leading to highly original outcomes.

ideas, seeking feedback, and revisiting the project until it feels complete, potentially struggling to finalize it due to a belief in continuous improvement.

**Support for Risk-Taking:** Creating environments that encourage and celebrate experimentation without fear of failure.

**Structured Reflection:** Encouraging reflection after revisions to understand when changes are sufficient (e.g., reflection journals, collaborative review sessions).

**Reflective Checkpoints:** Periodic evaluations of progress with peers or mentors to assess revisions and determine when to move forward.

In sum, effective self-regulation increases both the likelihood that people will experiment with creative tasks and their optimism about engaging in such tasks in the future.

## Conclusion

As discussed in this section, creative self-regulation helps to transform perceived creative agency into actual creative action. To behave creatively, individuals need the belief that they can do it (confidence), that it's worth doing (centrality), and that the risk is justified (creative risk-taking). But they also need knowledge, skills, and practical strategies. Creative self-regulation provides these strategies, enabling individuals to navigate the creative process effectively.

Creativity inherently involves uncertainty, which arises at every stage of the process, from idea generation to refining the final product (Beghetto, 2021b). This uncertainty serves as both a challenge and a catalyst for creativity. Creative self-regulation helps individuals manage uncertainty by reframing challenges as opportunities and sustaining motivation over time (Zielińska & Karwowski, 2022).

This often requires emotional regulation strategies such as tolerating ambiguity, maintaining resilience in the face of setbacks, and reframing negative experiences in a positive light. For example, a self-regulated individual might view the ambiguity of an open-ended task not as a source of anxiety but as an opportunity for exploration.

Creative self-regulation draws on several key mechanisms: *planning* (setting goals and breaking tasks into manageable steps), *monitoring* (assessing progress and adapting strategies), *emotional regulation* (managing emotions like frustration and anxiety), and *reflection* (reviewing outcomes to guide future efforts).

Supporting these mechanisms through targeted interventions (e.g., self-regulation prompts) can significantly enhance creative performance. Educators and managers, for example, can introduce goal setting, strategic planning, and self-reflection techniques to help students and employees regulate their creative processes more effectively. Providing constructive feedback and opportunities for reflection further fosters creative self-regulation, motivating individuals to refine their strategies and persist through challenges.

## 6 Creative Behavior as Agentic Action: Theoretical Propositions

Having discussed the four core facets of creative agency, we now discuss how they can be combined into an updated version of the CBAA model (Karwowski & Beghetto, 2019). We then offer ten theoretical propositions that can guide future theory and research on creative agency.

CBAA departs from traditional, cognitive, and often linear models of creativity by emphasizing the intentional, agentic nature of creative actions. At its core, the CBAA model challenges the notion that creativity is merely a product of spontaneous bursts of inspiration or that it is reducible to cognitive mechanisms.

Rather, the CBAA model posits that creative behavior results from deliberate, goal-directed action shaped by an individual's perceptions, motivations, emotions, and contextual factors. The idea of "agentic action" is central here. Drawing heavily upon Bandura's (1982, 1997) concept of human agency, we believe that people are active participants in their creative endeavors, agents capable of influencing their environment and shaping their creative outcomes.

The initial iteration of the CBAA (Karwowski & Beghetto, 2019) model focused on creative potential, confidence, centrality, and behavior. These four elements served as a framework for understanding how creative actions are initiated, conducted, and sustained. However, our elaborated view on creative agency presented in this Element highlights the role played by two additional agentic factors: creative risk-taking and creative self-regulation. Given this, the CBAA model requires extension and refinement.

Next, we summarize ten main propositions critical for the CBAA model. Some (Propositions 1–5) are drawn from the original version of the CBAA. Others (Propositions 6–8) are based on recent research conducted in our labs and presented in this Element. The final two propositions (9–10) are hypotheses that have yet to be empirically tested. This list should not be viewed as exhaustive and final. On the contrary, the CBAA model is a broad and evolving framework for understanding creative action.

## Ten CBAA-Related Propositions

***Proposition 1. Creative Potential Is Not Sufficient for Creative Action and Achievement.*** The first proposition critical to the CBAA model is based on the observation that the links between *creative potential* and *creative activity* or *achievement* tend to be inconsistent and modest at best (Karwowski & Beghetto, 2019). Creative potential includes processes such as divergent thinking, remote associations, metaphorical and analogical thinking, and other cognitive processes relevant to creative thought.

Although foundational studies show that creative abilities can translate into achievement (Plucker, 1999), this translation is neither automatic nor straightforward (Benedek, 2024). A recent meta-analysis (Said-Metwaly et al., 2024), for example, found that the relationship between measures of potential and achievement is statistically significant but weak ($r = 0.18$).

Beyond simple linear, average-based relationships, there is still merit to the claim that creative potential plays a key role in creative achievement. Specifically, creative potential seems to be a necessary but not sufficient condition for successful creative outcomes. When potential is low, creative achievement is unlikely (though not impossible). Conversely, high potential alone does not guarantee success.

This reasoning has been empirically supported in the case of intelligence (Karwowski et al., 2016, 2017), and creative potential appears to follow a similar logic. The key question, however, is: What factors help to convert creative potential into creative action? The CBAA model posits that creative confidence and centrality play crucial roles in this process. Creative confidence is theorized to mediate the link between potential and behavior, while creative centrality is proposed to moderate it. We explain the reasoning behind these mechanisms in Propositions 2 and 3.

***Proposition 2. Creative Confidence Mediates the "Potential-Action" Link.*** Creative confidence is theorized as a mediator in the potential-action chain. In other words, the CBAA model posits that people's creative potential influences their level of confidence, which in turn supports creative activity and achievement.

The theorized "path a" of the mediation model assumes that potential shapes confidence. That is, individuals with higher creative abilities and skills tend to develop higher creative confidence. Why might this be the case? At least three mechanisms help explain how higher potential contributes to greater confidence.

The first mechanism is metacognitive. There is a positive, albeit weak-to-moderate, relationship between creative abilities and the ability to recognize creativity in one's own and others' ideas (Guo et al., 2022). More creative people tend to be more aware of their creative strengths. Although this relationship is far from perfect (recall the Dunning–Kruger effect, which is less pronounced in the case of creativity, Lebuda et al., 2024), creative people, overall and on average, may be considered "doubly skilled" (Silvia, 2008): they can effectively generate creative ideas and accurately recognize the creativity of their ideas. This metacognitive awareness may be one reason why potential shapes confidence.

The second mechanism is experiential. As Bandura (1997) explained, mastery experiences (past successes) build self-efficacy. More creatively skilled individuals are more likely to work through setbacks, solve problems, and succeed in creative tasks. These experiences build confidence, as they demonstrate to people that they are capable of creative achievement.

The third mechanism is social in origin. Bandura's theory highlights that self-efficacy is shaped by social persuasion, such as the messages individuals receive from significant others. More creative people are more likely to receive positive feedback from their peers (McKay et al., 2017), parents (Jankowska et al., 2024; Jankowska & Karwowski, 2019), and teachers (Karwowski et al., 2015), which can help bolster their creative confidence.

These three factors – metacognitive (awareness of one's own creativity), experiential (successes in the past), and social (positive feedback) – do not form an exhaustive list of all potential mechanisms of linking potential and confidence. They are also not mutually exclusive. In fact, they likely interact and reinforce one another to build creative confidence.

What empirical evidence supports this relationship? Meta-analytical estimates show significant, albeit somewhat weak, correlations between creative potential and confidence (Haase et al., 2018). Demonstrating causal links is challenging, as creative potential is difficult to manipulate directly. However, one recent study (Wiśniewska & Karwowski, in press) used a unique design to examine the effects of creativity training.

Participants' creative abilities and confidence were measured twice in experimental and control groups before and after the training. The training was highly effective. Participants in the experimental group showed substantial gains in creative ability, while the control group did not. Creative confidence also increased in the experimental group, though the effect was smaller.

A more complex effect was also observed, which is particularly relevant to the present discussion. A mediation model revealed that the change in creative confidence was fully mediated by the change in creative potential. In other words, training strengthened participants' creative abilities, and this improvement in abilities (in the experimental group) fully accounted for the rise in their creative confidence. Although preliminary, this *Abilities-Shape-Confidence Effect* aligns with the causal logic proposed in the CBAA.

Further indirect support for a causal relationship between potential and confidence comes from two preregistered experiments. These experiments tested people's divergent thinking and confidence by manipulating the instructions given to participants (Wojtycka et al., under review).

The classic "be creative" effect in the creativity literature (Harrington, 1975) has been shown to increase creativity compared to other prompts like "be fluent." While this effect may be partly metacognitive, this manipulation can be viewed as a way of activating creative thinking. The key question is not only whether this activation improves creativity, as many studies have shown (e.g., Wei et al., 2024), but whether it also boosts creative confidence.

In both preregistered experiments, the "be creative" instruction was highly effective in strengthening participants' creative ideas (Cohen's $ds > 1$) and also increased their creative confidence. This effect was moderated by participants' metacognitive accuracy. In other words, confidence gains were stronger among participants who were better at judging how creative their own ideas were. These experimental findings provide further support for the posited causal link between creative potential and confidence.

There is also a second mediational path (the "b") in the potential-confidence-behavior chain. This path posits a causal relationship between confidence and creative action. Indeed, individuals' creative confidence can change the likelihood of creative outcomes (e.g., Haase et al., 2018), but most of this evidence comes from correlational, between-person studies.

Causal studies remain rare but informative. For instance, a daily diary intervention that used simple motivational prompts to support students' confidence increased their engagement in creative activities (Zielińska et al., 2022b). Similarly, a recent two-year longitudinal study with Japanese adolescents (Ishiguro et al., 2025) demonstrated higher levels of creative behavior led to higher creative confidence, which then predicted creative behavior six months later.

Taken together, these findings suggest that creative confidence is both a cause and effect of creative activity and achievements, in line with social cognitive theory (Bandura, 1982). However, the level of analysis matters. Most studies have examined confidence-action relationships at between-person level, correlating trait-level creative confidence with activity, or achievement in large samples of participants (Lebuda et al., 2021). Far fewer have tested within-person effects (Sitzmann & Yeo, 2013), and the results of such analytical approaches are mixed.

Specifically, the path from activity to confidence seems to be largely independent of the design and level of analysis (i.e., between or within-person). However, the confidence-performance associations at the within-person level (see, e.g., Beattie et al., 2016), vary greatly, with results showing positive, null, or even negative associations (see Sitzmann & Yeo, 2013, for a meta-analysis).

Notably, these studies rarely explore creative confidence and creative performance. Rather, most focus on people's general or job-specific self-efficacy in relationship to their organizational performance. Studies directly exploring within-person effects or both between- and within-person associations are rare (Karwowski et al., 2019a). A recent diary study (Zielińska & Karwowski, under review), however, is an exception.

Results from the diary study demonstrated robust correlations between confidence and activity at both between- and within-person levels. Lagged effects revealed that creative activity on one day predicted next-day confidence, but the reverse effect was not observed.

The initial CBAA model was theorized as a between-person framework (but see Beghetto & Karwowski, 2017). However, we recognize that to further develop our understanding and model of creative agency, it is necessary to study the confidence-action links at both within- and between-person levels. Within-person analyses can untangle more dynamic, intraindividual processes that unfold over time, "unfreezing" creativity (Beghetto & Karwowski, 2019) and capturing the more fluid (rather than fixed) nature of self-beliefs (Karwowski et al., 2019a).

Some researchers have offered explanations for the mixed findings regarding the within-person links between confidence and performance. When negative relationships were observed, Vancouver et al. (2002) offered an important explanation: As a person's confidence increases during a task, they may reduce their effort because they believe the task is easier than it actually is. While it might seem logical to reduce effort on an "easy" task to conserve resources, this overconfidence can lead to poorer performance on complex tasks. This is why Bandura and Locke (2003) emphasized that proper within-person tests are needed to test the causal links between confidence and performance on realistic tasks of increasing difficulty.

Finally, the assertion that confidence builds performance is supported by empirical studies that manipulate people's agentic factors and assess how such manipulation translates into their creative performance. Across several preregistered experiments, Zielińska and Karwowski (2024) activated individuals' confidence and centrality by, for example, manipulating the order of instruments. The experimental group was first provided with items measuring confidence and centrality, and then, after such activation, presented with performance tasks. The control group started with performance tasks or asked participants to reflect on why creativity matters for them (centrality condition), what makes them creative (confidence condition), or a combination of various activations.

The results of these experiments showed significant effects that ranged from $d = 0.13$ when participants' creativity was measured with a story task to $d = 0.60$ when the alternate uses task was applied. The meta-analytically obtained average was $d = 0.34$ (95% CI: 0.21–0.48), a small-to-medium effect (Cohen, 1992). This is comparable to the average meta-analytically obtained effects of creativity training on participants' creativity (Sio & Lortie-Forgues, 2024), which ranged from $d = 0.29$ to $d = 0.32$ (when corrected for statistical artifacts).

In other words, the brief and subtle activation of participants' creative agency factors resulted in gains similar to those achieved through more prolonged and intensive creativity programs. Thus, not only does activation of confidence and centrality have practical consequences for creative action, but it also supports the CBAA model's claim: agency factors, particularly creative confidence, play a causal role in shaping creative performance.

The next three propositions (3, 4, and 5) are related to the role of creative centrality in the CBAA model and the relationships between confidence and centrality. More specifically, although the links between confidence and centrality are usually quite strong, it is hypothesized that they play complementary yet distinctive roles in activating and sustaining creative action. We turn now to that reasoning.

***Proposition 3. Creative Centrality Moderates the "Potential-Action" Link.*** As the CBAA model posited and research demonstrates (Karwowski & Beghetto, 2019), creative centrality plays a peculiar role in the agentic system. On the one hand, centrality is a robust and consistent predictor of behavior. Even more importantly, however, the level of centrality qualifies the links between potential and behavior.

This moderation effect was consistently observed in cross-sectional and longitudinal studies, with virtually null links between potential and performance among people who do not value creativity or do not consider it essential for their identity (low centrality) and positive, significant relationships among those who treat creativity as a vital part of themselves.

More detailed analyses have shown that this moderation effect might not be linear, that is, what particularly matters is the situation when creative centrality is low or very low (e.g., Karwowski and Beghetto, 2019, found that creative centrality at or below the 30th percentile is particularly problematic) because people with such low centrality do not fulfill their potential.

As illustrated in Figure 4, even very high cognitive potential is fruitless if not accompanied by at least moderate (or preferably high) valuing of creativity. In a sense, therefore, creative centrality might be considered a necessary condition of performance. When it is low, the chances that potential will be fulfilled are negligible.

***Proposition 4. Centrality Moderates the "Potential-Confidence-Behavior" Mediation.*** The vital role of creative centrality is further strengthened by the fact that it not only qualifies the "potential-behavior" links (Proposition 3) but also moderates the "b" path, that is, the causal relationship between confidence and behavior. This second moderation role is, in fact, two-fold. On the one hand, centrality strengthens the links between confidence and behavior (see Karwowski & Beghetto, 2019, Study 2).

On the other hand, the CBAA model hypothesizes what is technically called a "moderated mediation," that is, centrality moderates the whole "potential-confidence-behavior" mediational chain. In other words, what

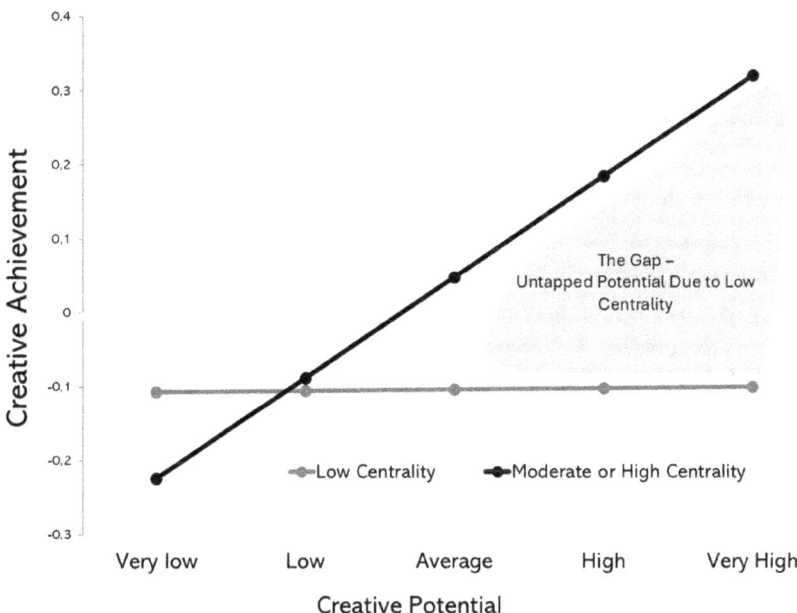

**Figure 4** Moderating effects of creative centrality in potential-achievement

we discussed in detail under "Proposition 2" is further qualified by people's creative centrality.

This moderated mediation was consistently replicated across two cross-sectional and one longitudinal study (Karwowski & Beghetto, 2019), showing that the indirect effect of potential on behavior as mediated by confidence is stronger among people with solid creative centrality, and this mediation did not occur among those whose centrality was low. This again emphasizes the vital role centrality plays as the trigger of the whole agency loop.

***Proposition 5. Confidence and Centrality Are Reciprocally and Dynamically Intertwined.*** The fifth proposition highlights the dynamic links between confidence and centrality, two initial elements of the CBAA model.

Although they are usually quite strongly correlated, this correlation might be caused – at least partly – by the common method variance issue, since both confidence and centrality are typically measured by different items of the same instrument (most often the Short Scale of Creative Self; Karwowski et al., 2018; Zielińska et al., 2022a). However, there are also empirical and theoretical arguments to consider their interrelations at the more dynamic level.

Theoretically, there are reasons to consider centrality a cause of confidence, but the reverse is also true.

First, since centrality strongly relates to a person's identity and creativity's place in self-perception, it generalizes into broad spheres of a person's functioning. Therefore, those who care about creativity and consider it essential are more likely to develop the conviction (accurate or not) that they can function creatively (Tierney & Farmer, 2011).

However, the reverse is also true. Perhaps the links from confidence to centrality are even stronger (Karwowski, 2016) than those from centrality to confidence. Indeed, two longitudinal studies demonstrated that confidence might boost centrality, so people start valuing those spheres of their functioning in which they feel competent (Karwowski, 2016). Therefore, the reciprocal loop between these two elements of creative agency seems well-corroborated.

Creative risk-taking and creative self-regulation were not included in the original CBAA model. However, the growing number of studies summarized in this Element, and the theoretical role of those two factors for agentic functioning, calls for their inclusion in a more elaborated version of the model. We see at least two findings that inform the following propositions (6 and 7).

***Proposition 6. Creative Risk-Taking Predicts Behavior and Moderates the "Confidence-Behavior" Links.*** Although the specific role played by creative risk-taking requires further research (see also Section 4), one investigation (Beghetto et al., 2021) provides a compelling case to consider risk-taking as both an independent predictor of creative behavior and a factor that moderates the relationship between confidence and activity and achievement in various domains.

As previously discussed with centrality (see Proposition 3), a very low proclivity toward risk-taking (about 2 standard deviations below the mean) had two effects. First, it eliminated the link between confidence and creative activity/achievement in arts and science. Second, when examining overall creative achievement, these individuals with very low risk-taking showed a negative, rather than positive, relationship between their creative confidence and achievement.

Thus, although the role played by risk-taking in creative behavior warrants future investigations, what we have learned so far highlights this factor's importance for activating creative activity.

***Proposition 7. Creative Self-Regulation Is Driven by and Drives Confidence.*** As we explained in Section 5, research shows that not only does confidence shape self-regulation, but the reverse is also true.

Confidence as a prerequisite for self-regulation is among the foundational axioms of social cognitive theory (Bandura, 1982, 1997). More confident people self-regulate better because of what they have learned, thanks to a richer repertoire of more advanced mental strategies, and the bolder goals they posit.

As demonstrated elsewhere (Zielińska & Karwowski, under review), supporting students' creative self-regulation not only results in more creative effects but also builds students' creative confidence. Therefore, confidence shapes self-regulation, but self-regulation also results in stronger confidence.

Moreover, there are some arguments to expect that confidence built by self-regulation might be (although this is a hypothesis to be tested) more accurate and closely aligned with performance. As we already discussed, sometimes confidence, especially overestimation, demobilizes personal resources rather than increasing motivation (Vancouver et al., 2002).

However, when confidence is self-regulated and activity-driven (rather than self-enhanced from ego motives), it is expected to be more closely related to the task and activity context, resulting in appropriate reactions. When confidence increases thanks to improved self-regulation, it might result in more enduring, long-lasting creative engagement.

***Proposition 8. Creative Self-Regulation Makes Behavior Effective.*** The eighth proposition, the final one among those that have been at least partially confirmed in empirical studies, posits that creative self-regulation not only predicts the intensity of engaging in creative activity but also the degree to which that activity translates into achievement.

As illustrated elsewhere (Zielińska et al., 2023, see also Section 5), although activity is necessary for accomplishments, effective self-regulation strengthens the links between activity and achievement. Two additional CBAA-related propositions regarding risk-taking and creative self-regulation propositions await empirical testing and validation. We briefly discuss them next.

***Proposition 9. Confidence Shapes Risk-Taking.*** Although risk-taking was demonstrated to moderate the relationship between confidence and creative activity, there are also arguments for considering confidence as a factor that shapes risk-taking tendencies.

Based on what we know about creatively self-efficacious people, chances are that they will exercise their confidence by examining nonobvious ways of behavior and testing unsafe routes. Indeed, it seems that creative risk-taking requires substantial creative confidence. Correlations between these constructs are robust ($r = 0.42$, Beghetto et al., 2021), yet causal links remain to be established. Both experimental and longitudinal investigations with measures going beyond static self-report instruments are particularly welcome to uncover these associations.

***Proposition 10. Self-Regulation Empowers Potential.*** The tenth and final CBAA-related proposition relates to what could be considered an apparent yet overlooked relationship. We posit that creative self-regulation – like creative centrality – is the factor that unlocks creative potential and transfers it into observable outcomes.

Therefore, we expect a moderation-like relationship (interaction) between potential and self-regulation to strengthen the chances for effective creative behavior. Again, however, details matter, and new investigations are not only necessary to test if this hypothesized moderation occurs at all but also to determine its character. For example, do more creatively skilled people additionally benefit when their self-regulation is high (synergy between potential and self-regulation), or perhaps does creative self-regulation instead counterbalance lower levels of creative potential? These and other questions have yet to be answered.

The overview we presented, with a particular focus on two new categories absent in the initial CBAA model, creative risk-taking and creative self-regulation, led to the extended incarnation of the CBAA (Figure 5). Categories in gray boxes are original factors covered by the initial version of the model.

Black arrows denote relationships postulated and confirmed at the early stages of the CBAA model's development (although often more robust empirical tests were obtained afterward). Gray arrows demonstrate the links theorized based on empirical results discussed in this section. Finally, the dotted gray lines are related to the hypothetical effects that await empirical tests.[3]

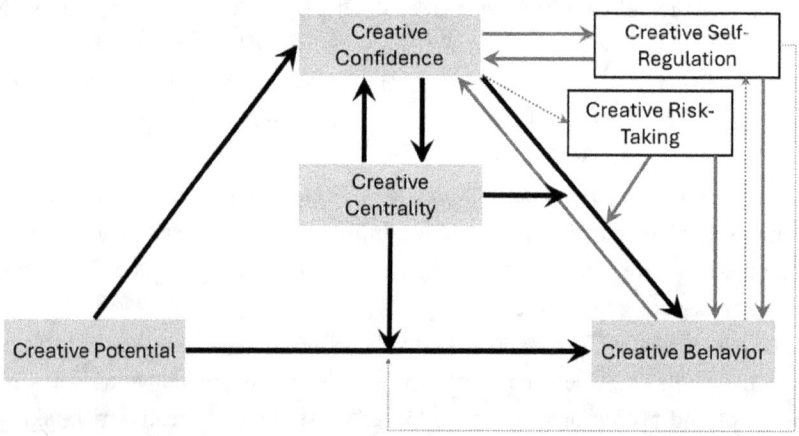

**Figure 5** The revised creative behavior as agentic action model

---

[3] Dotted gray lines primarily refer to our Propositions 9 and 10. The one exception is the direct relationship between creative behavior and creative self-regulation, suggested by an anonymous reviewer. Indeed, some recent works (Ivcevic Pringle, 2025; Sawyer, 2025) provide a compelling case that more experienced (and accomplished) creators are better in self-regulating their actions. A precise mechanism of why it is the case, is to be uncovered by future works.

## Conclusion

The CBAA model focuses on the intentional, agent-driven nature of creative acts. Moving away from traditional views of creativity as either spontaneous or purely cognitive, the CBAA framework asserts that creative behaviors result from goal-directed behaviors shaped by individuals' motivations, perceptions, and the broader context. Inspired by Bandura's human agency theory, the model views individuals as active actors influencing their creative outcomes, positioning creativity as an agentic action.

The original CBAA model was built upon four key pillars: creative potential, creative confidence, creative centrality, and creative behavior. Together, these elements provided a framework to understand how creative actions are initiated and sustained. However, as research on creative agency evolved, two additional factors – creative risk-taking and creative self-regulation – were identified as vital additions to the model. Creative risk-taking, for instance, moderates the relationship between confidence and creative achievement. Creative self-regulation, meanwhile, influences the effectiveness of creative behaviors and helps sustain them.

Among the most critical aspects for the future development of the CBAA model is the consideration of creative goals. Understanding how individuals formulate creative goals, the boldness of these goals, and the role of agency in goal setting are key areas for refinement. Creative goals are not simply aspirations; they reflect an individual's agency and capacity to act creatively. Investigating how factors like creative confidence and self-regulation influence the boldness and complexity of goal formulation will provide valuable insights into the creative process.

Another promising extension of the CBAA model involves explorations in collaborative agency. This includes group dynamics, where teams work creatively, and collaborative interactions between humans and GenAI. As GenAI becomes more integrated into creative processes, understanding how individuals or groups co-create with AI systems and how agency is distributed in such collaborations will be critical to further expanding the CBAA framework (Faiella et al., 2025; Reich & Teeny, 2025; Zielińska & Karwowski, in press).

In conclusion, the CBAA model offers a dynamic and evolving view of creativity, emphasizing the agentic nature of creative behaviors. By incorporating insights on creative goal setting and exploring the nuances of collaborative agency, the model is well-positioned to further our understanding of creativity in both individual and collective contexts. These future directions will refine the theoretical foundations of the CBAA model and open new avenues for empirical investigation, especially considering technological advancements in GenAI.

## 7 Supporting Creative Agency: Practical Questions and Strategies

Transforming creative potential into creative behavior requires cultivating creative agency. As we have discussed, this is essential across human activity, enabling meaningful personal experiences, making creative contributions to others, solving complex societal problems, and ensuring human survival.

This concluding section transitions from theory to practice, offering actionable insights. We outline common questions and offer practical strategies to foster the core beliefs of creative agency (i.e., creative confidence, creative centrality, creative risk-taking, and creative self-regulation). Given the broad relevance of these concepts, the questions and strategies are framed for broad applicability.

However, when illustrating these strategies, we have focused our examples on educational contexts. Educators (from K-12 through higher education) are uniquely positioned to influence the long-term creative trajectories of young people, making this a critical domain for application (Anderson, 2024; McDiarmid et al., in press). Grounding the examples in teaching practice also allows for consistent and concrete illustrations of implementing these principles. We invite readers to view these educational scenarios as specific illustrations of broader principles that can be adapted to workplaces, studios, communities, or personal growth initiatives.

The strategies are drawn from a growing body of research (Karwowski et al., 2020; Lin-Siegler et al., 2016), theory (Beghetto, 2023), and meta-analyses (Karwowski et al., 2022). Some represent established approaches, while others are promising directions needing further real-world testing and refinement by practitioners in their specific contexts (Zielińska et al., 2022; Zielińska & Karwowski, under review).

### Creative Confidence

*1. How can creative confidence be fostered in individuals or groups?*

- **Strategy:** Promote the idea that creativity is not a fixed trait but can be developed through effort, practice, learning from mistakes, and embracing challenges.

- **Example:** Ms. Johnson, an art teacher, starts her classes by displaying famous artists' early works alongside their masterpieces. She discusses how these artists evolved, emphasizing that skill and creativity improve with dedication. Similarly, she encourages students to view their creative journey by celebrating progress rather than just outcomes.

## 2. How can I address creativity misconceptions and stereotypes?

- **Strategy:** Challenge misconceptions that creativity is only for certain people or domains.
- **Example:** Ms. Johnson holds a class debate on "Only artists are creative." Through guided discussion, students explore and address stereotypes, broadening their understanding of who can be creative and reinforcing that creativity is accessible to all.

## 3. How can I provide opportunities for mastery experiences in creativity?

- **Strategy:** Design challenging yet achievable tasks, allowing people to experience success in creative endeavors.
- **Example:** In a science class, Mr. Lee assigns a project where students design a simple invention to solve a common problem. He ensures the problems students select are feasible and the required materials are accessible. Students gain confidence in their creative abilities when they successfully create their inventions.

## 4. How can I use modeling to promote creativity?

- **Strategy:** Highlight examples of peers or colleagues demonstrating creativity, reinforcing that it is attainable.
- **Example:** Ms. Nguyen invites former students who excelled in last year's school innovation fair to share their projects and experiences with the class. Hearing from relatable and successful peers can help current students envision themselves achieving similar success.

## 5. How can I leverage Generative AI to support, not replace, human creativity?

- **Strategy:** Guide people to use GenAI tools as creative partners to generate possibilities and develop their ideas while emphasizing that they retain creative ownership.
- **Example:** Mr. Evans introduces a GenAI image tool. Students use it to explore visual representations of characters from a story they are writing, trying different prompts and styles. He emphasizes that the AI is a tool to help them visualize, not to create their final characters. Instead, they are expected to use the AI for inspiration and to create the final images themselves.

## 6. How can I offer constructive feedback on creative work?

- **Strategy:** Give feedback that is specific, positive, and focused on the process as well as the product, supporting people's creative confidence.
- **Example:** After a creative writing assignment, Ms. Patel provides individualized comments highlighting each student's unique ideas and

effective use of language. She also suggests areas for improvement, encouraging students to refine their work without diminishing their confidence.

## Creative Centrality

*1. How can I create a context that values creativity?*

- **Strategy:** Establish norms and values prioritizing creativity, making it a shared identity among teams and groups.
- **Example:** Mr. O'Neil starts the school year by collaborating with students to develop a "Creativity Contract" for the classroom. The contract includes embracing new ideas, supporting peers' creative efforts, and taking intellectual risks. This collective agreement fosters a sense of belonging centered around creativity.

*2. How can I model creative identity?*

- **Strategy:** Demonstrate your own creative identity and share personal experiences involving creativity.
- **Example:** Ms. Davis, a science teacher passionate about photography, shares her photos related to scientific concepts discussed in class. She talks about how her creative pursuits enhance her understanding and enjoyment of science, inspiring students to see creativity as a valuable part of their identities.

*3. How can I highlight the value of creativity in various domains?*

- **Strategy:** Discuss how creativity is valuable in multiple aspects of life, including careers, relationships, and personal growth.
- **Example:** During career week, Mr. Chen organizes sessions where professionals from diverse fields (e.g., engineering, entrepreneurship, and healthcare) share how creativity is essential in their work. This broadens students' understanding of creativity's importance beyond traditional creative industries.

*4. How can I connect creativity to individual interests and cultures?*

- **Strategy:** Acknowledge and incorporate people's cultural backgrounds and personal interests into creative activities.
- **Example:** Mr. Lopez invites students to create projects that reflect their cultural heritage, such as traditional art forms, music, or storytelling. This validates their backgrounds and weaves creativity into their sense of identity.

**5. How can I promote self-reflection on creative centrality?**
- **Strategy:** Encourage people to reflect on how creativity relates to their self-concept and future aspirations.
- **Example:** Ms. Williams introduces journaling prompts like "What does being creative mean to me?" or "How do I use creativity in my daily life?" Regular reflection helps students internalize creativity as a key component of their identity.

**6. How can I celebrate creative role models?**
- **Strategy:** Introduce people to diverse creative figures who exemplify how creativity shapes identity.
- **Example:** Ms. Kim includes biographical studies of innovators, artists, and thinkers from various backgrounds in her curriculum. By learning about these individuals' lives and how creativity was central to their identities, students find inspiration and relatable models.

## Creative Risk-Taking

**1. How can I create a safe environment for risk-taking?**
- **Strategy:** Foster a culture where experimentation is valued, and mistakes are seen as learning opportunities.
- **Example:** During a group activity, Mr. Rodriguez emphasizes the importance of sharing different perspectives and that making mistakes is part of learning. He models this by sharing unconventional ideas and openly discussing what can be learned from less successful attempts.

**2. How can I help people learn how to assess the costs and benefits of taking creative risks?**
- **Strategy:** Provide opportunities for people to analyze creative risks taken by others and reflect on their own risk-taking experiences. Provide experiences and scenarios that involve engaging with the uncertainty of ill-defined problems to help people learn how to judge risks and persist under states of uncertainty.
- **Example:** Before starting a design project that involves engaging with and resolving uncertainty, Ms. Jones facilitates a class discussion analyzing famous inventions. Students discuss both the potential benefits (e.g., solving a problem, improving lives) and the potential costs (e.g., financial investment, time commitment, potential for failure) associated with bringing these inventions to life. Later, after students complete their designs, they reflect on how they felt about engaging with the uncertainty of ill-defined problems,

the risks they took, the perceived costs and benefits, how long it took them to identify viable solutions, and what they learned from the experience.

### 3. How can I provide time for creative exploration?

- **Strategy:** Allocate time specifically for creative thinking and experimentation without the pressure of evaluation.
- **Example:** Every Friday, Ms. Thompson designates "Innovation Hour," where students can work on passion projects related to the subject matter. This dedicated time allows them to explore ideas, receive supportive feedback, and develop their creative confidence and willingness to experiment.

### 4. How can I use collaborative learning to enhance creativity?

- **Strategy:** Design group activities that promote sharing ideas and peer support, fostering a sense of safety for creative risk-taking.
- **Example:** Mr. Davis organizes small groups in a music class where students compose and perform original pieces. Collaborating with peers allows students to gain confidence as they contribute unique ideas, learn from one another, and feel more comfortable taking creative risks in a supportive environment.

### 5. How can I connect creative risk-taking to real-world contexts?

- **Strategy:** Show how creativity is valuable beyond the immediate context can enhance people's willingness to take creative risks.
- **Example:** Ms. Lee invites local entrepreneurs and artists to speak about how creativity impacts their work. Understanding the real-world applications of creativity helps students appreciate their own potential contributions and strengthens their commitment to creative risk-taking.

### 6. How can I provide feedback to encourage creative risk-taking?

- **Strategy:** When providing feedback, emphasize the value of experimentation, the learning that comes from trying new approaches, and the importance of viewing failures as opportunities for growth rather than focusing solely on the outcome.
- **Example:** After a creative writing assignment where students were encouraged to experiment with different genres, Mr. Quinn praises students for their willingness to try a style outside their comfort zone, even if their writing can still be improved through additional work. He highlights how experimentation led to interesting ideas and language choices, reinforcing the value of taking creative risks.

## Creative Self-Regulation

1. ***How can I incorporate self-regulation strategies to support the creative process?***
   - **Strategy:** Integrate explicit instruction and practice of self-regulation strategies into creative tasks, connecting these skills to both the creative process and real-world applications, and provide opportunities for people to personalize and reflect on their learning.
   - **Example:** When teaching a unit on historical fiction, Mr. Thompson introduces self-regulation strategies as essential tools for this type of writing. He describes strategies like setting writing goals, developing outlines, conducting meticulous research, evaluating sources, revising drafts, and managing emotional responses to feedback. Students then practice these strategies while researching and writing their own historical fiction stories, reflecting on their process in writing journals and discussing the effectiveness of different approaches.

2. ***How can I help people develop effective goal-setting, planning, and visualization skills for creative projects?***
   - **Strategy:** Guide people to set realistic and achievable creative goals, break down projects into manageable steps, visualize successful completion, and develop strategies for monitoring progress, adapting plans, and anticipating challenges.
   - **Example:** At the beginning of a photography unit, Ms. Ramirez introduces the SMART goal framework (Specific, Measurable, Achievable, Relevant, Time-bound) and helps students develop project proposals. A student might set a SMART goal like, "Capture a series of five photographs showcasing "Urban Textures" using natural lighting within two weeks." Students then outline specific steps, visualize themselves successfully completing each step (e.g., finding ideal locations, mastering camera settings), and anticipate potential challenges (e.g., inclement weather, difficulty finding suitable textures). Ms. Ramirez encourages students to document these visualized steps and foreseen challenges in their project journals. Throughout the project, she facilitates reflection on their progress, encouraging them to adjust their plans, celebrate accomplishments, and connect their visualized outcomes to their actual experiences, fostering self-regulation, creative confidence, and problem-solving skills.

3. **How can I help people develop metacognitive awareness and control over their creative processes?**
   - **Strategy:** Encourage individuals to reflect on their thinking processes, identify their creative strengths and weaknesses, and develop strategies for overcoming creative challenges.
   - **Example:** After a brainstorming session for a design project, Mr. Chen asks students to map out their idea-generation process. They discuss different brainstorming techniques, analyze which ones were most effective for them, and identify any creative blocks they encountered. This metacognitive reflection helps them become more aware of their creative thinking and develop strategies to regulate their ideation process.

4. **How can I promote self-monitoring, reflection, and adaptive adjustments during creative projects?**
   - **Strategy:** Provide tools and opportunities for people to track their progress, reflect on their creative choices, identify areas for improvement, and adjust their strategy accordingly.
   - **Example:** Ms. Jones provides students with "Creative Process Journals," where they document their project goals, track daily progress, reflect on challenges and successes, and analyze the effectiveness of their strategies. She regularly reviews the journals with students, providing feedback and encouraging them to adjust their approach based on their reflections.

5. **How can I help people develop emotional regulation and resilience during creative work?**
   - **Strategy:** Teach techniques for managing emotions like frustration, anxiety, and disappointment, emphasizing the importance of perseverance and a growth mindset.
   - **Example:** Before assigning a challenging coding project, Mr. Garcia teaches students about growth mindset and strategies they can use (e.g., asking for help, taking a break) to help regulate negative emotions they might experience when facing difficulties and setbacks in their project. He encourages students to use these techniques throughout the project and normalizes the experience of setbacks, framing them as opportunities for learning and growth.

6. **How can I help students develop effective time management and organizational skills for creative projects?**
   - **Strategy:** Provide people with tools, strategies, and support for planning, prioritizing, and managing their time effectively during creative projects, gradually releasing responsibility as they gain proficiency.

- **Example:** Ms. Rodriguez introduces students to project management techniques like creating timelines, breaking down tasks, and setting deadlines. She initially provides templates and checklists but gradually encourages students to develop their own organizational systems, fostering independence and ownership over their creative work.

By addressing these practical questions and implementing the suggested strategies, educators, leaders, mentors, and individuals can cultivate environments that nurture creative agency. We encourage all readers, including teachers testing these approaches with their students, managers fostering innovation in teams, artists pushing creative boundaries, and individuals pursuing personal growth, to experiment with these strategies. The goal is to promote creative confidence, support creative centrality beliefs, encourage creative risk-taking, and equip individuals with creative self-regulation skills.

As practitioners thoughtfully integrate these approaches into their specific contexts, they can help individuals develop their creative potential. This involves empowering people, particularly students, to view themselves as confident, capable, and agentic creators within and beyond formal settings, ultimately translating their creative potential into meaningful creative action in diverse learning, life, and work areas.

# References

Amabile, T. M. (1996). *Creativity in context: Update to the social psychology of creativity.* Westview.

Amabile, T. M., Conti, R., Coon, H., Lazenby, J., & Herron, M. (1996). Assessing the work environment for creativity. *Academy of Management Journal, 39*(5), 1154–1184. https://doi.org/10.2307/256995.

Amabile, T. M., Hennessey, B. A., & Grossman, B. S. (1986). Social influences on creativity: The effects of contracted-for reward. *Journal of Personality and Social Psychology, 50*(1), 14–23. https://doi.org/10.1037/0022-3514.50.1.14.

Amabile, T. M., & Kramer, S. J. (2011). *The progress principle*: Using small wins to ignite joy, engagement, and creativity at work. Harvard Business Review Press.

Ambrose, D. (2015). Borrowing insights from other disciplines to strengthen the conceptual foundations for gifted education. *International Journal for Talent Development and Creativity, 3*, 33–57.

Ames, C. (1992). Classrooms: Goals, structures, and student motivation. *Journal of Educational Psychology, 84*(3), 261–271. https://doi.org/10.1037/0022-0663.84.3.261.

Anderson, R. C. (2024). Creative development as an agentic process: Five distinct trajectories of divergent thinking originality across early adolescence. *Learning and Individual Differences, 112*, 102448. https://doi.org/10.1016/j.lindif.2024.102448.

Anderson, R. C. (2025). A longitudinal teacher case study on the development of creative self-regulation and agency. *Journal of Creative Behavior, 59*, 1–18, e1534. https://doi.org/10.1002/jocb.1534.

Baer, J. (2015). *Domain specificity of creativity.* Academic Press.

Baird, B., Smallwood, J., Mrazek, M. D. et al. (2012). Inspired by distraction: Mind wandering facilitates creative incubation. *Psychological Science, 23*(10), 1117–1122. https://doi.org/10.1177/0956797612446024.

Bandura, A. (1982). Self-efficacy mechanism in human agency. *American Psychologist, 37*(2), 122–147. https://doi.org/10.1037/0003-066X.37.2.122.

Bandura, A. (1986). *Social foundations of thought and action*: A social cognitive theory. Prentice-Hall.

Bandura, A. (1997). *Self-efficacy*: The exercise of control. WH Freeman.

Bandura, A. (2001). Social cognitive theory: An agentic perspective. *Annual Review of Psychology, 52*, 1–26. https://doi.org/10.1146/annurev.psych.52.1.1.

Bandura, A. (2006). Guide to construction of self-efficacy scales. In F. Pajares & T. Urdan (Eds.), *Self-efficacy beliefs of adolescents* (Vol. 5, pp. 307–337). Information Age.

Bandura, A. (2012). On the functional properties of perceived self-efficacy revisited. *Journal of Management*, *38*(1), 9–44. https://doi.org/10.1177/0149206311410606.

Bandura, A., & Locke, E. A. (2003). Negative self-efficacy and goal effects revisited. *Journal of Applied Psychology*, *88*(1), 87–99. https://doi.org/10.1037/0021-9010.88.1.87.

Barron, F. (1969). *Creative person and creative process*. Holt, Rinehart, & Winston.

Baumeister, R. F. (2008). Free will in scientific psychology. *Perspectives on Psychological Science*, *3*(1), 14–19. https://doi.org/10.1111/j.1745-6916.2008.00057.x.

Baumeister, R. F., Bratslavsky, E., Finkenauer, C., & Vohs, K. D. (2001). Bad is stronger than good. *Review of General Psychology*, *5*(4), 323–370.

Baumeister, R. F., Bratslavsky, E., Muraven, M., & Tice, D. M. (1998). Ego depletion: Is the active self a limited resource? *Journal of Personality and Social Psychology*, *74*, 1252–1265. https://psycnet.apa.org/doi/10.1037/0022-3514.74.5.1252.

Beattie, S., Woodman, T., Fakehy, M., & Dempsey, C. (2016). The role of performance feedback on the self-efficacy–performance relationship. *Sport, Exercise, and Performance Psychology*, *5*(1), 1–13. https://doi.org/10.1037/spy0000051.

Beghetto, R. A. (2006). Creative self-efficacy: Correlates in middle and secondary students. *Creativity Research Journal*, *18*(4), 447–457. https://doi.org/10.1207/s15326934crj1804_4.

Beghetto, R. A. (2013). *Killing ideas softly? The promise and perils of creativity in the classroom*. Charlotte, NC: Information Age Publishing.

Beghetto, R. A. (2014). Creative mortification: An initial exploration. *Psychology of Aesthetics, Creativity, and the Arts*, *8*(3), 266–276. https://doi.org/10.1037/a0036618.

Beghetto, R. A. (2019). *Beautiful risks: Having the courage to teach and learn creatively*. Rowman & Littlefield.

Beghetto, R. A. (2020). Creative self-efficacy. In M. A. Runco & S. R. Pritzker (Eds.), *Encyclopedia of creativity* (3rd ed.) (pp. 322–327). Elsevier. https://doi.org/10.1016/B978-0-12-809324-5.23789-9.

Beghetto, R. A. (2021a). Creative identity development in classrooms. In J. Hoffmann, S. Russ, & J. C. Kaufman (Eds.), *Cambridge handbook of lifespan development in creativity* (pp. 395–414). Cambridge University Press. https://doi.org/10.1017/9781108755726.023.

Beghetto, R. A. (2021b). There is no creativity without uncertainty: Dubito Ergo Creatio. *Journal of Creativity, 31*, 1–5. https://doi.org/10.1016/j.yjoc.2021.100005.

Beghetto, R. A. (2023). *Uncertainty x design: Educating for possible futures.* Cambridge University Press.

Beghetto, R. A., & Dilley, A. E. (2016). Creative aspirations or pipe dreams? Toward understanding creative mortification in children and adolescents. *New Directions for Child and Adolescent Development, 151*, 85–95. https://doi.org/10.1002/cad.20150.

Beghetto, R. A., & Karwowski, M. (2017). Toward untangling creative self-beliefs. In M. Karwowski & J. C. Kaufman (Eds.), *The creative self* (pp. 3–22). Academic Press. http://dx.doi.org/10.1016/B978-0-12-809790-8.00001-7.

Beghetto, R. A., & Karwowski, M. (2019). Unfreezing creativity: A dynamic, micro-longitudinal approach. In R. A. Beghetto & G. Corazza (Eds.), *Dynamic perspectives on creativity* (pp. 67–85). Springer. https://doi.org/10.1007/978-3-319-99163-4_2.

Beghetto, R. A., & Karwowski, M. (2023). Creative self-beliefs: From creative potential to creative action. In R. Reiter-Palmon & S. Hunter (Eds.), *Handbook of organizational creativity: Individual and group level influences* (2nd ed., pp. 179–193). Academic Press. https://doi.org/10.1016/B978-0-323-91840-4.00010-4.

Beghetto, R. A., Karwowski, M., & Reiter-Palmon, R. (2021). Intellectual risk taking: A moderating link between creative confidence and creative behavior? *Psychology of Aesthetics, Creativity, and the Arts, 15*(4), 637–644. https://doi.org/10.1037/aca0000323.

Beghetto, R. A., & Mangion, M. (2023). Beyond "cold" creative metacognition: Toward a more integrated framework. *Physics of Life Reviews, 47*, 200–202. https://doi.org/10.1016/j.plrev.2023.10.021.

Benedek, M. (2024). On the relationship between creative potential and creative achievement: Challenges and future directions. *Learning and Individual Differences, 110*, 102424. https://doi.org/10.1016/j.lindif.2024.102424.

Benedek, M., & Jauk, E. (2019). Creativity and cognitive control. In J. C. Kaufman & R. J. Sternberg (Eds.), *The Cambridge handbook of creativity* (2nd ed., pp. 200–223). Cambridge University Press. https://doi.org/10.1017/9781316979839.012.

Benedek, M., Karstendiek, M., Ceh, S. M. et al. (2021). Creativity myths: Prevalence and correlates of misconceptions on creativity. *Personality and Individual Differences, 182*, 111068. https://doi.org/10.1016/j.paid.2021.111068.

Benedek, M., & Lebuda, I. (2024). Managing your muse: Exploring three levels of metacognitive control in creative ideation. *Creativity Research Journal*, 1–12. https://doi.org/10.1080/10400419.2024.2347770.

Berkovich, I. (2020). Something borrowed, something blue: Reflections on theory borrowing in educational administration research. *Journal of Educational Administration*, *58*, 749–760. https://doi.org/10.1108/JEA-03-2020-0058.

Bink, M. L., & Marsh, R. L. (2000). Cognitive regularities in creative activity. *Review of General Psychology*, *4*(1), 59–78. https://doi.org/10.1037/1089-2680.4.1.59.

Blair, C. S., & Mumford, M. D. (2007). Errors in idea evaluation: Preference for the unoriginal? *Journal of Creative Behavior*, *41*, 197–222. http://dx.doi.org/10.1002/j.2162-6057.2007.tb01288.x.

Bown, O., & McCormack, J. (2011). Creative agency: A clearer goal for artificial life in the arts. In G. Kampis, I. Karsai, & E. Szathmáry (Eds.), *Advances in artificial life: Darwin meets von Neumann. ECAL 2009. Lecture Notes in Computer Science*, vol. 5778. Springer. https://doi.org/10.1007/978-3-642-21314-4_32.

Breakwell, G. M. (2014). *The psychology of risk* (2nd ed.). Cambridge University Press.

Brehm, J. (1966). *A theory of psychological reactance*. Academic Press.

Byrnes, J. P. (1998). *The nature and development of decision-making: A self-regulation model*. Psychology Press. http://dx.doi.org/10.4324/9780203726495.

Callan, G. L., Rubenstein, L. D., Ridgley, L. M., Speirs Neumeister, K., & Hernández Finch, M. E. (2021). Self-regulated learning as a cyclical process and predictor of creative problem-solving. *Educational Psychology*, *41*(9), 1139–1159. https://doi.org/10.1080/01443410.2021.1913575.

Carson, S. H., Peterson, J. B., & Higgins, D. M. (2005). Reliability, validity, and factor structure of the creative achievement questionnaire. *Creativity Research Journal*, *17*(1), 37–50. https://doi.org/10.1207/s15326934crj1701_4.

Charyton, C., Snelbecker, G. E., Rahman, M. A., & Elliott, J. O. (2013). College students' creative attributes as a predictor of cognitive risk tolerance. *Psychology of Aesthetics, Creativity, and the Arts*, *7*(4), 350–357. https://doi.org/10.1037/a0032706.

Christoff, K., Irving, Z. C., Fox, K. C. R., Spreng, R. N., & Andrews-Hanna, J. R. (2016). Mind-wandering as spontaneous thought: A dynamic framework. *Nature Reviews Neuroscience*, *17*(11), 718–731. https://doi.org/10.1038/nrn.2016.113.

Churchland, P. M. (1981). Eliminative materialism and the propositional attitudes. *The Journal of Philosophy, 78*(2), 67–90.

Churchland, P. S. (1986). *Neurophilosophy: Toward a unified science of the mind-brain*. MIT Press.

Cohen, J. (1992). A power primer. *Psychological Bulletin, 112*(1), 155–159. https://doi.org/10.1037/0033-2909.112.1.155.

Crepaldi, M., Fusi, G., Cancer, A., Iannello, P., & Rusconi, M. L. (2024). The bidirectional relationship between risk and creativity: A systematic review. *TPM-Testing, Psychometrics, Methodology in Applied Psychology, 31*(1), 41–57.

Denrell, J. (2007). Adaptive learning and risk taking. *Psychological Review, 114* (1), 177–187. https://doi.org/10.1037/0033-295X.114.1.177.

Dewett, T. (2006). Exploring the role of risk in employee creativity. *Journal of Creative Behavior, 40*(1), 27–45. https://doi.org/10.1002/j.2162-6057.2006 .tb01265.x.

Diedrich, J., Jauk, E., Silvia, P. J. et al. (2018). Assessment of real-life creativity: The Inventory of Creative Activities and Achievements (ICAA). *Psychology of Aesthetics, Creativity, and the Arts, 12*(3), 304–316. https://doi.org/10.1037/ aca0000137.

Dollinger, S. J., Burke, P. A., & Gump, N. W. (2007). Creativity and values. *Creativity Research Journal, 19*(2–3), 91–103. https://doi.org/10.1080/ 10400410701395028.

Eccles, J. S., & Wigfield, A. (2002). Motivational beliefs, values, and goals. *Annual Review of Psychology, 53*(1), 109–132. https://doi.org/10.1146/ annurev.psych.53.100901.135153.

Edmondson, A. C. (1999). Psychological safety and learning behavior in work teams. *Administrative Science Quarterly, 44*(2), 350–383. https://doi.org/ 10.2307/2666999.

Faiella, A., Zielińska, A., Karwowski, M., & Corazza, G. E. (2025). Am I still creative? The effect of artificial intelligence on creative self-beliefs. *Journal of Creative Behavior, 59*, e70011. https://doi.org/10.1002/jocb.70011.

Farmer, S. M., & Tierney, P. (2017). Considering creative self-efficacy: Its current state and ideas for future inquiry. In M. Karwowski & J. C. Kaufman (Eds.), *The creative self* (pp. 23–47). Academic Press. https://doi.org/10.1016/B978-0-12-809790-8.00002-9.

Ford, C. M. (1996). A theory of individual creative action in multiple social domains. *The Academy of Management Review, 21*(4), 1112–1142. https:// doi.org/10.2307/259166.

Forestier, C., de Chanaleilles, M., Boisgontier, M. P., & Chalabaev, A. (2022). From ego depletion to self-control fatigue: A review of criticisms along with new perspectives for the investigation and replication of a multicomponent phenomenon. *Motivation Science*, *8*(1), 19–32. https://doi.org/10.1037/mot0000262.

Fürst, G., Ghisletta, P., & Lubart, T. (2017). An experimental study of the creative process in writing. *Psychology of Aesthetics, Creativity, and the Arts*, *11*(2), 202–215. https://doi.org/10.1037/aca0000106.

Getzels, J. W., & Jackson, P. W. (1962). *Creativity and intelligence: Explorations with gifted students*. John Wiley & Sons.

Glaveanu, V., Lubart, T., Bonnardel, N. et al. (2013). Creativity as action: Findings from five creative domains. *Frontiers in Psychology*, *4*, 1–14. https://doi.org/10.3389/fpsyg.2013.00176.

Glăveanu, V. P. (2013). Rewriting the language of creativity: The five A's framework. *Review of General Psychology*, *17*(1), 69–81. https://doi.org/10.1037/a0029528.

Glăveanu, V. P., & Kaufman, J. C. (2019). Creativity: A historical perspective. In J. C. Kaufman & R. J. Sternberg (Eds.), *The Cambridge handbook of creativity* (2nd ed., pp. 9–26). Cambridge University Press. https://doi.org/10.1017/9781316979839.003.

Groenendijk, T., Janssen, T., Rijlaarsdam, G., & Van Den Bergh, H. (2013). Learning to be creative. The effects of observational learning on students' design products and processes. *Learning and Instruction*, *28*, 35–47. https://doi.org/10.1016/j.learninstruc.2013.05.001.

Grohman, M. G., Ivcevic, Z., Silvia, P., & Kaufman, S. B. (2017). The role of passion and persistence in creativity. *Psychology of Aesthetics, Creativity, and the Arts*, *11*(4), 376–385. https://doi.org/10.1037/aca0000121.

Guilford, J. P. (1950). Creativity. *American Psychologist*, *5*, 444–454.

Guo, Y., Lin, S., Acar, S. et al. (2022). Divergent thinking and evaluative skill: A meta-analysis. *Journal of Creative Behavior*, *56*(3), 432–448. https://doi.org/10.1002/jocb.539.

Haase, J., Hoff, E. V., Hanel, P. H., & Innes-Ker, Å. (2018). A meta-analysis of the relation between creative self-efficacy and different creativity measurements. *Creativity Research Journal*, *30*(1), 1–16. https://doi.org/10.1080/10400419.2018.1411436.

Haefele, J. W. (1962). *Creativity and innovation*. Chapman & Hall.

Hagger, M. S., Chatzisarantis, N. L. D., Alberts, H. et al. (2016). A multilab preregistered replication of the ego-depletion effect. *Perspectives on Psychological Science*, *11*(4), 546–573. https://doi.org/10.1177/1745691616652873.

Harada, T. (2020). The effects of risk-taking, exploitation, and exploration on creativity. *PloS One*, *15*(7), e0235698. https://doi.org/10.1371/journal.pone.0235698.

Harrington, D. M. (1975). Effects of explicit instructions to "be creative" on the psychological meaning of divergent thinking test scores. *Journal of Personality*, *43*(3), 434–454. https://doi.org/10.1111/j.1467-6494.1975.tb00715.x.

Harris D. (2021). *Creative agency*. Palgrave.

Harris, D. X. (2023). Non-binary possibilities of creative agency. *Possibility Studies & Society*, *1*(1–2), 99–104. https://doi.org/10.1177/27538699231166485.

Helson, R. (1996). In search of the creative personality. *Creativity Research Journal*, *9*, 295–306.

Hitlin, S. (2003). Values as the core of personal identity: Drawing links between two theories of self. *Social Psychology Quarterly*, *66*(2), 118–137. https://doi.org/10.2307/1519843.

Hocevar, D. (1979). *The development of the Creative Behavior Inventory*. Paper presented at the annual meeting of the Rocky Mountain Psychological Association, Las Vegas, NV (ERIC Document Reproduction Service No. ED 170 350), April.

Huang, X., Chi-Kin Lee, J., & Yang, X. (2019). What really counts? Investigating the effects of creative role identity and self-efficacy on teachers' attitudes towards the implementation of teaching for creativity. *Teaching and Teacher Education*, *84*, 57–65. https://doi.org/10.1016/j.tate.2019.04.017.

Ishiguro, C., Matsumoto, K., Akata, T., & Okada, T. (2025). The relationship between creative self-concept and activities of Japanese junior high and high school students: A two-year longitudinal study. *Thinking Skills and Creativity*, *57*, 101831, https://doi.org/10.1016/j.tsc.2025.101831.

Ivcevic, Z., Grossman, E. R., Cotter, K. N., & Nusbaum, E. (2024). Self-regulation of creativity: Toward measuring strategies of creative action. *Creativity Research Journal*, *36*(3), 491–507. https://doi.org/10.1080/10400419.2023.2226494.

Ivcevic, Z., & Hoffmann, J. (2019). Emotions and creativity: From process to person and product. In J. C. Kaufman & R. J. Sternberg (Eds.), *The Cambridge handbook of creativity* (2nd ed., pp. 273–295). Cambridge University Press. https://doi.org/10.1017/9781316979839.015.

Ivcevic, Z., & Nusbaum, E. C. (2017). From having an idea to doing something with it: Self-regulation for creativity. In M. Karwowski & J. C. Kaufman (Eds.), *The creative self* (pp. 343–365). Academic Press. https://doi.org/10.1016/B978-0-12-809790-8.00020-0.

Ivcevic Pringle, Z. (2025). *The creativity choice: The science of making decisions to turn ideas into action*. PublicAffairs.

Jankowska, D. M., Czerwonka, M., Lebuda, I., & Karwowski, M. (2018). Exploring the creative process: Integrating psychometric and eye-tracking approaches. *Frontiers in Psychology*, *9*, 1–12, 1931. https://doi.org/10.3389/fpsyg.2018.01931.

Jankowska, D. M., & Karwowski, M. (2019). Family factors and development of creative thinking. *Personality and Individual Differences*, *142*, 202–206. https://doi.org/10.1016/j.paid.2018.07.030.

Jankowska, D. M., Lebuda, I., & Gralewski, J. (2024). Creating home: Socioeconomic status and home environment as predictors of family climate for creativity. *Thinking Skills and Creativity*, *52*, 101511. https://doi.org/10.1016/j.tsc.2024.101511.

Jose, T. (1970). Convergent-divergent thinking abilities and risk-taking in children. *Philippine Journal of Psychology*, *3*(1), 22–35.

Kahneman, D., & Tversky, A. (1979). Prospect theory: An analysis of decision under risk. *Econometrica*, *47*(2), 263–292.

Kaplan, A. (2008). Clarifying metacognition, self-regulation, and self-regulated learning: What's the purpose? *Educational Psychology Review*, *20*(4), 477–484. https://doi.org/10.1007/s10648-008-9087-2.

Karoly, P. (1993). Mechanisms of self-regulation: A systems view. *Annual Review of Psychology*, *44*(1), 23–52. https://doi.org/10.1146/annurev.ps.44.020193.000323.

Karwowski, M. (2011). It doesn't hurt to ask … But sometimes it hurts to believe: Polish students' creative self-efficacy and its predictors. *Psychology of Aesthetics, Creativity, and the Arts*, *5*(2), 154–164, https://doi.org/10.1037/a0021427.

Karwowski, M. (2012). Did curiosity kill the cat? Relationship between trait curiosity, creative self-efficacy and creative personal identity. *Europe's Journal of Psychology*, *8*(4), 547–558. https://doi.org/10.5964/ejop.v8i4.513.

Karwowski, M. (2014). Creative mindsets: Measurement, correlates, consequences. *Psychology of Aesthetics, Creativity, and the Arts*, *8*(1), 62–70. https://doi.org/10.1037/a0034898.

Karwowski, M. (2016). The dynamics of creative self-concept: Changes and reciprocal relations between creative self-efficacy and creative personal identity. *Creativity Research Journal*, *28*(1), 99–104. https://doi.org/10.1080/10400419.2016.1125254.

Karwowski, M., & Beghetto, R. A. (2019). Creative behavior as agentic action. *Psychology of Aesthetics, Creativity, and the Arts*, *13*(4), 402–415. https://doi.org/10.1037/aca0000190.

Karwowski, M., Czerwonka, M., Lebuda, I., Jankowska, D. M., & Gajda, A. (2020). Does thinking about Einstein make people entity theorists? Examining the malleability of creative mindsets. *Psychology of Aesthetics, Creativity, and the Arts*, *14*(3), 361–366. https://doi.org/10.1037/aca0000226.

Karwowski, M., Dul, J., Gralewski, J. et al. (2016). Is creativity without intelligence possible? A necessary condition analysis. *Intelligence*, *57*, 105–117.

Karwowski, M., Gralewski, J., & Szumski, G. (2015). Teachers' effect on students' creative self-beliefs is moderated by students' gender. *Learning and Individual Differences*, *44*, 1–8. https://doi.org/10.1016/j.lindif.2015.10.001.

Karwowski, M., Han, M. H., & Beghetto, R. A. (2019a). Toward dynamizing the measurement of creative confidence beliefs. *Psychology of Aesthetics, Creativity, and the Arts*, *13*(2), 193–202. https://doi.org/10.1037/aca0000229.

Karwowski, M., Kaufman, J. C., Lebuda, I., Szumski, G., & Firkowska-Mankiewicz, A. (2017). Intelligence in childhood and creative achievements in middle-age: The necessary condition approach. *Intelligence*, *64*, 36–44. https://doi.org/10.1016/j.intell.2017.07.001.

Karwowski, M., & Lebuda, I. (2017). Creative self-concept: A surface characteristic of creative personality. In G. J. Feist, R. Reiter-Palmon, & J. C. Kaufman (Eds.), *The Cambridge handbook of creativity and personality research* (pp. 84–101). Cambridge University Press. https://doi.org/10.1017/9781316228036.006.

Karwowski, M., Lebuda, I., & Beghetto, R. A. (2019b). Creative self-beliefs. In J. C. Kaufman & R. J. Sternberg (Eds.), *The Cambridge handbook of creativity* (2nd ed., pp. 396–417). Cambridge University Press. https://doi.org/10.1017/9781316979839.021.

Karwowski, M., Lebuda, I., & Wiśniewska, E. (2018). Measuring creative self-efficacy and creative personal identity. *The International Journal of Creativity & Problem Solving*, *28*(1), 45–57.

Karwowski, M., Lebuda, I., Wisniewska, E., & Gralewski, J. (2013). Big five personality traits as the predictors of creative self-efficacy and creative personal identity: Does gender matter? *Journal of Creative Behavior*, *47*(3), 215–232. https://doi.org/10.1002/jocb.32.

Karwowski, M., Royston, R. P., & Reiter-Palmon, R. (2019c). Exploring creative mindsets: Variable and person-centered approaches. *Psychology of Aesthetics, Creativity, and the Arts*, *13*(1), 36–48. https://doi.org/10.1037/aca0000170.

Karwowski, M., & Zielińska, A. (2024). Be curious: Strategic curiosity drives creativity. *Behavioral and Brain Sciences*, *47*, 42–44. https://doi.org/10.1017/S0140525X23003412.

Karwowski, M., Zielińska, A., & Jankowska, D. M. (2022). Democratizing creativity by enhancing imagery and agency: A review and meta-analysis. *Review of Research in Education*, *46*(1), 229–263. https://doi.org/10.3102/0091732X221084337.

Kaufman, J. C. (2016). *Creativity 101* (2nd ed.). Springer. http://dx.doi.org/10.1891/9780826129536.

Kaufman, J. C. (2023). *The creativity advantage*. Cambridge University Press.

Kaufman, J. C., & Beghetto, R. A. (2009). Beyond big and little: The four c model of creativity. *Review of General Psychology*, *13*(1), 1–12. https://doi.org/10.1037/a0013688.

Kaufman, J. C., & Beghetto, R. A. (2013). In praise of Clark Kent: Creative meta-cognition and the importance of teaching kids when (not) to be creative. *Roeper Review*, *35*, 155–165. https://doi/10.1080/02783193.2013.799413.

Lebuda, I., & Benedek, M. (2023). A systematic framework of creative metacognition. *Physics of Life Reviews*, *46*, 161–181. https://doi.org/10.1016/j.plrev.2023.07.002.

Lebuda, I., & Benedek, M. (2025). Contributions of metacognition to creative performance and behavior. *The Journal of Creative Behavior*, *59*(1), e652. https://doi.org/10.1002/jocb.652.

Lebuda, I., Hofer, G., Rominger, C., & Benedek, M. (2024). No strong support for a Dunning–Kruger effect in creativity: Analyses of self-assessment in absolute and relative terms. *Scientific Reports*, *14*(1), 1–11, 11883. https://doi.org/10.1038/s41598-024-61042-1.

Lebuda, I., Zielińska, A., & Karwowski, M. (2021). On surface and core predictors of real-life creativity. *Thinking Skills and Creativity*, *42*, 100973. https://doi.org/10.1016/j.tsc.2021.100973.

Lin-Siegler, X., Ahn, J. N., Chen, J., Fang, F.-F. A., & Luna-Lucero, M. (2016). Even Einstein struggled: Effects of learning about great scientists' struggles on high school students' motivation to learn science. *Journal of Educational Psychology*, *108*(3), 314–328. https://doi.org/10.1037/edu0000092.

List, C. (2023). Agential possibilities. *Possibility Studies & Society*, *1*(4), 461–470. https://doi.org/10.1177/27538699231200093.

Lubart, T. (Ed.). (2018). *The creative process*. Palgrave Macmillan. https://doi.org/10.1057/978-1-137-50563-7.

Lubart, T. I., & Sternberg, R. J. (1998). Creativity across time and place: Life span and cross-cultural perspectives. *High Ability Studies*, *9*(1), 59–74. https://doi.org/10.1080/1359813980090105.

Maehr, M. L., & Midgley, C. (1991). Enhancing student motivation: A schoolwide approach. *Educational Psychologist*, *26*(3-4), 399–427. https://doi.org/10.1207/s15326985ep2603&4_9.

Malanchini, M., Engelhardt, L. E., Grotzinger, A. D., Harden, K. P., & Tucker-Drob, E. M. (2019). "Same but different": Associations between multiple aspects of self-regulation, cognition, and academic abilities. *Journal of Personality and Social Psychology*, *117*(6), 1164–1188. https://doi.org/10.1037/pspp0000224.

Marsh, H. W., Pekrun, R., Parker, P. D. et al. (2019). The murky distinction between self-concept and self-efficacy: Beware of lurking jingle-jangle fallacies. *Journal of Educational Psychology*, *111*(2), 331–353. https://doi.org/10.1037/edu0000281.

Mawang, L. L., Kigen, E. M., & Mutweleli, S. M. (2020). Achievement goal motivation and cognitive strategies as predictors of musical creativity among secondary school music students. *Psychology of Music*, *48*(3), 421–433. https://doi.org/10.1177/0305735618805837.

McDiarmid, W. G., Beghetto, R. A., & Zhao, Y. (in press). *Agents of impact: How education can empower students to change themselves, their communities, and their world*. Solution Tree Press.

McKay, A. S., Grygiel, P., & Karwowski, M. (2017). Connected to create: A social network analysis of friendship ties and creativity. *Psychology of Aesthetics, Creativity, and the Arts*, *11*(3), 284–294. https://doi.org/10.1037/aca0000117.

McVeigh, M., Valquaresma, A., & Karwowski, M. (2023). Fostering creative agency through screenwriting: An intervention. *Creativity Research Journal*, *35*(4), 749–762. https://doi.org/10.1080/10400419.2023.2168341.

Morris, C. W. (1956). *Varieties of human value*. University of Chicago Press.

Mumford, M. D., & Gustafson, S. B. (1988). Creativity syndrome: Integration, application, and innovation. *Psychological Bulletin*, *103*(1), 27–43. https://doi.org/10.1037/0033-2909.103.1.27.

Muraven, M. R., & Baumeister, R. F. (2000). Self-regulation and depletion of limited resources: Does self-control resemble a muscle? *Psychological Bulletin*, *126*, 247–259.

Niu, W., & Kaufman, J. C. (2013). Creativity of Chinese and American cultures: A synthetic analysis. *Journal of Creative Behavior*, *47*(1), 77–87. https://doi.org/10.1002/jocb.25.

O'Quin, K., & Besemer, S. P. (1999). Creative products. In M. A. Runco & S. Pritzker (Eds.), *Encyclopedia of creativity* (1st ed., pp. 413–422). Academic Press.

Pankove, E., & Kogan, N. (1968). Creative ability and risk-taking in elementary school children. *Journal of Personality*, *36*(3), 420–439. https://doi.org/10.1111/j.1467-6494.1968.tb01483.x.

Plucker, J. A. (1999). Is the proof in the pudding? Reanalyses of Torrance's (1958 to present) longitudinal data. *Creativity Research Journal, 12*(2), 103–114. https://doi.org/10.1207/s15326934crj1202_3.

Plucker, J. A., Beghetto, R. A., & Dow, G. T. (2004). Why isn't creativity more important to educational psychologists? Potentials, pitfalls, and future directions in creativity research. *Educational Psychologist, 39*(2), 83–96.

Plucker, J. A., & Runco, M. A. (1998). The death of creativity measurement has been greatly exaggerated: Current issues, recent advances, and future directions in creativity assessment. *Roeper Review, 21*(1), 36–39. https://doi.org/10.1080/02783199809553924.

Puryear, J. S., Kettler, T., & Rinn, A. N. (2017). Relationships of personality to differential conceptions of creativity: A systematic review. *Psychology of Aesthetics, Creativity, and the Arts, 11*(1), 59–68. https://doi.org/10.1037/aca0000079.

Putney, H., Silver, S., Silvia, P. J., Christensen, A. P., & Cotter, K. N. (2024). Why does creativity foster well-being? Autonomy, competence, and relatedness during everyday creative activities. *Journal of Research in Personality, 113*, 104552. https://doi.org/10.1016/j.jrp.2024.104552.

Raidl, M.-H., & Lubart, T. I. (2001). An empirical study of intuition and creativity. *Imagination, Cognition and Personality, 20*(3), 217–230. https://doi.org/10.2190/34qq-ex6n-tf8v-7u3n.

Reich, T., & Teeny, J. D. (2025). Does artificial intelligence cause artificial confidence? Generative artificial intelligence as an emerging social referent. *Journal of Personality and Social Psychology.* Advance online publication. https://dx.doi.org/10.1037/pspa0000450.

Reiter-Palmon, R., & Murugavel, V. (2018). The effect of problem construction on team process and creativity. *Frontiers in Psychology, 9*, 2098. https://doi.org/10.3389/fpsyg.2018.02098.

Rojas, J. P., & Tyler, K. M. (2018). Measuring the creative process: A psychometric examination of creative ideation and grit. *Creativity Research Journal, 30*(1), 29–40. https://doi.org/10.1080/10400419.2018.1411546.

Rubenstein, L. D., Callan, G. L., & Ridgley, L. M. (2018). Anchoring the creative process within a self-regulated learning framework: Inspiring assessment methods and future research. *Educational Psychology Review, 30*(3), 921–945. https://doi.org/10.1007/s10648-017-9431-5.

Rubenstein, L. D., Callan, G. L., Speirs Neumeister, K., Ridgley, L. M., & Hernández Finch, M. (2020). How problem identification strategies influence creativity outcomes. *Contemporary Educational Psychology, 60*, 101840. https://doi.org/10.1016/j.cedpsych.2020.101840.

Runco, M. A., & Jaeger, G. J. (2012). The standard definition of creativity. *Creativity Research Journal, 24*(1), 92–96.

Said-Metwaly, S., Taylor, C. L., Camarda, A., & Barbot, B. (2024). Divergent thinking and creative achievement – How strong is the link? An updated meta-analysis. *Psychology of Aesthetics, Creativity, and the Arts, 18*(5), 869–881. https://doi.org/10.1037/aca0000507.

Sapolsky, R. M. (2023). *Determined: Life without free will*. Random House.

Sawyer, R. K. (2012). *Explaining creativity: The science of human innovation* (2nd ed.). Oxford University Press.

Sawyer, R. K. (2025). *Learning to see: Inside the world's leading art and design schools*. MIT Press.

Schoggen, P. (1989). *Behavior settings: A revision and extension of Roger G. Barker's "ecological psychology."* Stanford University Press.

Schwartz, S. H. (1992). Universals in the content and structure of values: Theoretical advances and empirical tests in 20 countries. In M. P. Zanna (Ed.), *Advances in Experimental Social Psychology* (Vol. 25, pp. 1–26). Academic Press.

Schwartz, S. H. (1994). Are there universal aspects in the structure and content of human values? *Journal of Social Issues, 50*, 19–45.

Shen, W., Hommel, B., Yuan, Y., Chang, L., & Zhang, W. (2018). Risk-taking and creativity: Convergent, but not divergent thinking is better in low-risk takers. *Creativity Research Journal, 30*(2), 224–231. https://doi.org/10.1080/10400419.2018.1446852.

Silvia, P. J. (2008). Discernment and creativity: How well can people identify their most creative ideas? *Psychology of Aesthetics, Creativity, and the Arts, 2*(3), 139–146. https://doi.org/10.1037/1931-3896.2.3.139.

Silvia, P. J. (2018). Creativity is undefinable, controllable, and everywhere. In R. J. Sternberg & J. C. Kaufman (Eds.), *The nature of human creativity* (1st ed., pp. 291–301). Cambridge University Press. https://doi.org/10.1017/9781108185936.021.

Sio, U. N., & Lortie-Forgues, H. (2024). The impact of creativity training on creative performance: A meta-analytic review and critical evaluation of 5 decades of creativity training studies. *Psychological Bulletin, 150*(5), 554–585. https://doi.org/10.1037/bul0000432.

Sitzmann, T., & Yeo, G. (2013). A meta-analytic investigation of the within-person self-efficacy domain: Is self efficacy a product of past performance or a driver of future performance? *Personnel Psychology, 66*(3), 531–568. https://doi.org/10.1111/peps.12035.

Sternberg, R. J., & Karami, S. (2024). *Transformational creativity: Learning for a better future*. Palgrave.

Sternberg, R. J., & Lubart, T. I. (1995). *Defying the crowd: Cultivating creativity in a culture of conformity*. Free Press.

Tang, M., Werner, C., & Karwowski, M. (2016). Differences in creative mindset between Germany and Poland: The mediating effect of individualism and collectivism. *Thinking Skills and Creativity*, *21*, 31–40. https://doi.org/10.1016/j.tsc.2016.05.004.

Thomson, P., & Jaque, S. V. (2023). Ethnicity, creative identity, creative process, and adversity in college and community samples. *Journal of Creativity*, *33*(1), 100044. https://doi.org/10.1016/j.yjoc.2023.100044.

Tierney, P. (1997). The influence of cognitive climate on job satisfaction and creative efficacy. *Journal of Social Behavior & Personality*, *12*(4), 831–847.

Tierney, P., & Farmer, S. M. (2002). Creative self-efficacy: Its potential antecedents and relationship to creative performance. *Academy of Management Journal*, *45*(6), 1137–1148. https://doi.org/10.2307/3069429.

Tierney, P., & Farmer, S. M. (2011). Creative self-efficacy development and creative performance over time. *Journal of Applied Psychology*, *96*(2), 277–293. https://doi.org/10.1037/a0020952.

Tromp, C. (2024). Creativity from constraint: Exploration and exploitation. *Psychological Reports*, *127*(4), 1818–1843. https://doi.org/10.1177/00332941221114421.

Tyagi, V., Hanoch, Y., Hall, S. D., Runco, M., & Denham, S. L. (2017). The risky side of creativity: Domain specific risk-taking in creative individuals. *Frontiers in Psychology*, *8*, 1–9, 145. Doi: 10.3389/fpsyg.2017.00145.

Vallée-Tourangeau, F., & March, P. L. (2020). Insight out: Making creativity visible. *Journal of Creative Behavior*, *54*(4), 824–842. https://doi.org/10.1002/jocb.409.

Vancouver, J. B., Thompson, C. M., Tischner, E. C., & Putka, D. J. (2002). Two studies examining the negative effect of self-efficacy on performance. *Journal of Applied Psychology*, *87*(3), 506–516. https://doi.org/10.1037/0021-9010.87.3.506.

Vohs, K. D., & Schooler, J. W. (2008). The value of believing in free will: Encouraging a belief in determinism increases cheating. *Psychological Science*, *19*(1), 49–54. https://doi.org/10.1111/j.1467-9280.2008.02045.x

Vohs K. D., Baumeister R. F., Schmeichel B. J. et al. (2008). Making choices impairs subsequent self-control: A limited-resource account of decision making, self-regulation, and active initiative. *Journal of Personality and Social Psychology*, *94*, 883–898. https://doi.org/10.1037/0022-3514.94.5.883.

von Thienen, J., Meinel, C., & Corazza, G. E. (2017). A short theory of failure. *Electronic Colloquium on Design Thinking Research*, *17*, 1–5.

Wei, X., Shen, W., Long, H., & Lu, F. (2024). The power of the "be creative" instruction: A meta-analytical evaluation. *Learning and Motivation, 85,* 101945. https://doi.org/10.1016/j.lmot.2023.101945.

Weiss, S., Steger, D., Kaur, Y. et al. (2021). On the trail of creativity: Dimensionality of divergent thinking and its relation with cognitive abilities, personality, and insight. *European Journal of Personality, 35*(3), 291–314. https://doi.org/10.1002/per.2288.

Whitehead, A. N. (1978). *Process and reality: An essay in cosmology.* (Corrected edition, D. R. Griffin & D. W. Sherburne, Eds.). Free Press. (Original work published 1929).

Wiśniewska, E., & Karwowski, M. (in press). On the cognitive, metacognitive, and agentic effects of creativity training. *Thinking Skills and Creativity.*

Wojtycka, L., Zielińska, A., & Karwowski, M. (under review). How cognition and metacognition interact in explaining creative confidence. Manuscript submitted for publication.

Zandi, N., Karwowski, M., Forthmann, B., & Holling, H. (2025). How stable is the creative self-concept? A latent state-trait analysis. *Psychology of Aesthetics, Creativity, and the Arts, 19*(1), 101–111. https://doi.org/10.1037/aca0000521.

Zielińska, A., Forthmann, B., Lebuda, I., & Karwowski, M. (2025a). Self-regulation for creative activity: The same or different across domains? *Psychology of Aesthetics, Creativity, and the Arts, 19*(2), 307–328. https://dx.doi.org/10.1037/aca0000540.

Zielińska, A., & Karwowski, M. (2022). Living with uncertainty in the creative process: A self-regulatory perspective. In R. A. Beghetto & G. J. Jaeger (Eds.), *Uncertainty: A catalyst for creativity, learning and development* (pp. 81–102). Springer. https://doi.org/10.1007/978-3-030-98729-9_6.

Zielińska, A., & Karwowski, M. (2023). *Navigating the possible: Self-regulation of the anticipated creative action.* Paper presented at the 3rd Possibilities Study Network Conference, Dublin, July 21.

Zielińska, A., & Karwowski, M. (2024). *Unlocking creative potential: The effects of creative self-concept activation on creative performance.* Paper presented at APA Division 10's First Annual Research Conference, Denton TX, March 16.

Zielińska, A., & Karwowski, M. (under review). The dynamics of creative agency: Insights from two intensive diary studies on university students. *Manuscript submitted for publication.*

Zielińska, A., & Karwowski, M. (in press). Creative AI-gency: How AI elicits human creative potential. In M. J. Worwood & J. C. Kaufman (Eds.), *Generative artificial intelligence and creativity: Possibilities, precautions, and perspectives.* Academic Press.

Zielińska, A., Lebuda, I., Czerwonka, M., & Karwowski, M. (2025b). Self-regulation prompts improve creative performance. *Journal of Creative Behavior*, *59*(1), e674. https://doi.org/10.1002/jocb.674.

Zielińska, A., Lebuda, I., Gop, A., & Karwowski, M. (2024). Teachers as creative agents: How self-beliefs and self-regulation drive teachers' creative activity. *Contemporary Educational Psychology*, *77*, 102267. https://doi.org/10.1016/j.cedpsych.2024.102267.

Zielińska, A., Lebuda, I., Ivcevic, Z., & Karwowski, M. (2022). How adolescents develop and implement their ideas? On self-regulation of creative action. *Thinking Skills and Creativity*, *43*, 100998. https://doi.org/10.1016/j.tsc.2022.100998.

Zielińska, A., Lebuda, I., & Karwowski, M. (2022a). Scaling the creative self: An item response theory analysis of the Short Scale of Creative Self. *Creativity Research Journal*, *34*(4), 431–444. https://doi.org/10.1080/10400419.2022.2123139.

Zielińska, A., Lebuda, I., & Karwowski, M. (2022b). Simple yet wise? Students' creative engagement benefits from a daily intervention. *Translational Issues in Psychological Science*, *8*(1), 6–23. https://doi.org/10.1037/tps0000289.

Zielińska, A., Lebuda, I., & Karwowski, M. (2023). Dispositional self-regulation strengthens the links between creative activity and creative achievement. *Personality and Individual Differences*, *200*, 111894. https://doi.org/10.1016/j.paid.2022.111894.

Zimmerman, B. J. (1990). Self-regulated learning and academic achievement: An overview. *Educational Psychologist*, *25*(1), 3–17.

Zimmerman, B. J. (2000). Self-efficacy: An essential motive to learn. *Contemporary Educational Psychology*, *25*(1), 82–91. https://doi.org/10.1006/ceps.1999.1016.

Zhou, J., & George, J. M. (2001). When job dissatisfaction leads to creativity: Encouraging the expression of voice. *Academy of Management Journal*, *44*(4), 682–696. https://doi.org/10.2307/3069410.

# Author's Note

Generative AI tools (Google Gemini and OpenAI ChatGPT) were used to assist with copy-editing, refining examples, and enhancing clarity. All AI-generated suggestions were critically reviewed and edited by the authors. The authors take full responsibility for the accuracy and originality of the final manuscript.

# Creativity and Imagination

## Anna Abraham
*University of Georgia, USA*

Anna Abraham, Ph.D. is the E. Paul Torrance Professor at the University of Georgia, USA. Her educational and professional training has been within the disciplines of psychology and neuroscience, and she has worked across a diverse range of academic departments and institutions the world over, all of which have informed her cross-cultural and multidisciplinary focus. She has penned numerous publications including the 2018 book, *The Neuroscience of Creativity* (Cambridge University Press), and 2020 edited volume, *The Cambridge Handbook of the Imagination*. Her latest book is *The Creative Brain: Myths and Truths* (2024, MIT Press).

### About the Series

Cambridge Elements in Creativity and Imagination publishes original perspectives and insightful reviews of empirical research, methods, theories, or applications in the vast fields of creativity and the imagination. The series is particularly focused on showcasing novel, necessary and neglected perspectives.

# Cambridge Elements

# Creativity and Imagination

## Elements in the Series

*Prophets at a Tangent: How Art Shapes Social Imagination*
Geoff Mulgan

*Visions and Decisions: Imagination and Technique in Music Composition*
Bruce Adolphe

*Item-Response Theory for Creativity Measurement*
Nils Myszkowski

*Design Thinking and Other Approaches: How Different Disciplines See, Think and Act*
Nathan Crilly

*Connective Creativity: What Art Can Teach Us About Collaboration*
Austin Choi-Fitzpatrick and Gordon Hoople

*Landscapes of the Imagination*
Gerald C. Cupchik

*Outsight: Restoring the Role of Objects in Creative Problem Solving*
Frédéric Vallée-Tourangeau

*Narrative Creativity: An Introduction to How and Why*
Angus Fletcher and Mike Benveniste

*Mechanisms of Change and Creativity in Nature and Culture*
Arne Dietrich

*Psychodrama: A Creative Method to Survive and Thrive*
Hod Orkibi

*The Imagination Pulse: From Flickers to Firestorms in Reading*
Sarah Bro Trasmundi

*Creative Agency Unbound*
Ronald A. Beghetto and Maciej Karwowski

A full series listing is available at: www.cambridge.org/ECAI

For EU product safety concerns, contact us at Calle de José Abascal, 56–1°, 28003 Madrid, Spain or eugpsr@cambridge.org.

www.ingramcontent.com/pod-product-compliance
Lightning Source LLC
LaVergne TN
LVHW011850060526
838200LV00054B/4267